Going Global in the World Language Classroom

With this practical resource, you'll learn how to promote global readiness and build international connections in the world language classroom. Master educator Erin E.H. Austin shares original strategies to facilitate productive language learning and demonstrates how to foster a rigorous, inclusive, and enriching environment. Designed to improve student motivation and engagement, the book is a shift from teaching *about* the world to teaching *with* the world. You'll come away with plenty of inspiring and effective ways to not only invite the world into the classroom but also bring the classroom to the world and, in so doing, support an inviting classroom environment.

The book abounds with low-cost, ready-to-implement tools, activities, and lesson ideas. The approaches in this book include coordinating international and world language events at school, using online resources to connect students to new languages and cultures, and broadening student horizons through books and podcasts. Austin also offers ways that further develop students' global education through travel and study abroad opportunities. With this book, your students will become culturally literate, motivated language learners who will be ready to enter the global community and continue to learn from and with the world.

Erin E.H. Austin is a National Board Certified French teacher, a 2018 NEA Foundation Global Fellow, and the Colorado Congress of Foreign Language Teachers' 2023 Teacher of the Year.

Other Eye on Education Books
Available from Routledge
(www.routledge.com/eyeoneducation)

The Ultimate Guide to Selling Your Original World Language Resources: How to Open, Fill, and Grow a Successful Online Curriculum Store
Erin E.H. Austin

Sparking Creativity in the World Language Classroom: Strategies and Ideas to Build Your Students' Language Skills
Deborah Blaz and Tom Alsop

The World Language Teacher's Guide to Active Learning: Strategies and Activities for Increasing Student Engagement, 3rd Edition
Deborah Blaz

The Antiracist World Language Classroom
Krishauna Hines-Gaither and Cécile Accilien

Your World Language Classroom: Strategies for In-Person and Digital Instruction
Rachelle Dené Poth

Enlivening Instruction with Drama and Improv: A Guide for Second Language and World Language Teachers
Melisa Cahnmann-Taylor and Kathleen R. McGovern

Leading Your Language Program: Strategies for Design and Supervision, Even If You Don't Speak the Language
Catherine Ritz

Differentiated Assessment for Middle and High School Classrooms
Deborah Blaz

Activities, Games, and Assessment Strategies for the World Language Classroom, 2nd Edition
Amy Buttner Zimmer

Going Global in the World Language Classroom

Ideas, Strategies, and Resources for Teaching and Learning with the World

Erin E.H. Austin

Designed cover image: © Getty Images

First published 2024
by Routledge
605 Third Avenue, New York, NY 10158

and by Routledge
4 Park Square, Milton Park, Abingdon, Oxon, OX14 4RN

Routledge is an imprint of the Taylor & Francis Group, an informa business

© 2024 Erin E.H. Austin

The right of Erin E.H. Austin to be identified as author of this work has been asserted in accordance with sections 77 and 78 of the Copyright, Designs and Patents Act 1988.

All rights reserved. The purchase of this copyright material confers the right on the purchasing institution to photocopy or download pages which bear a copyright line at the bottom of the page. No other parts of this book may be reprinted or reproduced or utilised in any form or by any electronic, mechanical, or other means, now known or hereafter invented, including photocopying and recording, or in any information storage or retrieval system, without permission in writing from the publishers.

Trademark notice: Product or corporate names may be trademarks or registered trademarks, and are used only for identification and explanation without intent to infringe.

ISBN: 9781032470245 (hbk)
ISBN: 9781032467214 (pbk)
ISBN: 9781003384267 (ebk)

DOI: 10.4324/9781003384267

Typeset in Palatino
by codeMantra

Access the Support Material: www.routledge.com/9781032467214

*For my family:
my parents, who sacrificed for me to travel;
my grandparents, with whom I exchanged postcards from around
the world;
my sister, with whom I share a second language, useful for sharing secrets
in front of our parents;
and my husband and children, with whom I now globetrot*

Contents

Meet the Author ix
Acknowledgments xi
Foreword xiii
Preface xvii

SECTION 1
THE CASE FOR A GLOBAL CONNECTION PLAN 1

1 Understanding Global Education 3

2 Creating a Global Connection Plan 19

SECTION 2
LEVERAGING LOWER-COST OPTIONS 31

3 Hosting 33

4 World Language Storytime 43

5 World Language Day at _____ 50

6 Empatico 57

7 ePals 62

8 International Events in an International Baccalaureate Setting 67

9 International Student Panel 72

10 Video Options 76

11 Podcasts 84

12 Window Swap 88

13 City Walks 92

14 News in Slow _____ 98

15 Sustainable Development Goal Units 102

SECTION 3
LEVERAGING HIGHER-COST OPTIONS 105

16 Student Trips Abroad 107

17 Concordia Language Villages 117

18 Global Literature 122

19 Global Volunteers and Global Leaders 128

20 CIEE High School Summer Abroad 135

21 Virtual Reality 143

22 Forging Your Own Path 147

SECTION 4
THE WAY FORWARD 151

23 Increasing Our Own Global Competence 153

24 Converting the Naysayers 159

25 Igniting the Spark 165

Resources 167

Meet the Author

Erin E.H. Austin is a National Board Certified French teacher and the Colorado Congress of Foreign Language Teachers' 2023 Teacher of the Year. She began her teaching career in Minnesota in 2002, and she holds a BA in both French and Art Education, a MA in Curriculum and Instruction, and graduate certificates in French Studies and Gifted, Creative and Talented Education. In 2018, Ms. Austin was a NEA Foundation Global Fellow, which was the catalyst for her professional interest in Global Education and afforded the opportunity to be a contributing author in Dr. Fernando Reimer's book *Twelve Lessons to Open Classrooms and Minds to the World*. She has been featured on several education podcasts, and she presents nationally on global education. Although she loves living in beautiful Colorado with her family, she is constantly planning her next trip abroad.

Acknowledgments

I was first exposed to the concept of global education as a class of 2018 NEA Foundation Global Learning Fellow. That program enabled me to learn and, ultimately, write and present about global education, and it ignited a mid-career evolution that has been fascinating and fun. I'm forever indebted to Dr. Fernando Reimers, Harriet Sanford, Dr. Robert Adams Jr., and Kristen Shannon for their work with the fellows. I'm sure it was, at times, trying—leading adults is no easy task! Dr. Reimers lent his knowledgeable voice as a leader in the field to the foreword of this book, and there was no one better to provide opening inspiration. To all of my class of 2018 Global Learning fellows, thank you for your continued support! Keeping in touch online and knowing that there's a group that is continually sharing with each other and propelling this movement forward keeps me and my little world language piece of the puzzle moving.

I could not have contributed to the global education conversation or the world language profession with this book if it weren't for my family. My husband's patience with my constant "I think I'm going to try this thing..." quality of mine truly knows no bounds. He, Susan Austin, and Jana Hassler were wonderful for stepping in to help with the kids while I wrote.

The expertise of Mina Delgado, Dr. LJ Randolph, Dr. Sheldon Eakins, Sara Sneed, Justin Lee, Karen Adler, and the team at Routledge were also instrumental in this book coming to light. Dr. Eakins's "Leading Equity Podcast", in particular, provided support and inspiration in the equity portions of Sections 2 and 3.

Finally, I'm grateful to all of the incredible educators and the two former students who are featured in the Spotlight sections in this book. Their expertise and excitement about cultivating global competence motivates me. This is truly a national network of teachers doing the work of global education. Every year our ranks grow, and our message grows stronger. To Anne

Muske, Christine Littmann, Cinthia Johnson, Dr. Cori Hixon, Dr. Joe Underwood, Jo Dougherty, Joe Fontana, Dr. Frédérique Grim, Jean Girard, Magali Torres, Mary Beth Johnson, Matt Benson, Meghan Schumacher, Monica Bryant, Nico Henry, Peter Dola, Sam Russell, Shauna Anderson, Sunny Cordray, Tamara Ramirez-Torres, and Noah Zeichner: *thank you, merci, gracias, danke, arigatou gozaimasu.*

Foreword

We make sense of the world, largely, through language. The ability to name things, to represent the world in the symbolic system which is a language, allows us to comprehend the world more deeply, not just to *live in the world* but *to understand it*. A language, the foundation of thought, allows us to experiment with representations of the world, to formulate explanations, to imagine things that do not yet exist, and to create. But a language affords us an even more important power, the power to communicate with others, to access their thoughts, their explanations, and their imaginings. It allows us the possibility to understand others, to see the world through their eyes, and to collaborate with them. It is in this power to see the world through the eyes of others, to discover our shared humanity, that a language also enables us to improve the world. Because there are few improvements to our circumstances, to our communities, that can be achieved without collaboration with others, a language is therefore a central component of our *agency*.

As our capacity for discernment and agency are shaped by our linguistic community, our very sense of belonging, our views of who are our in-groups and out-groups are also shaped by the language we share. Expanding our ability to communicate in other languages is therefore a way to expand our community, our sense of belonging to a larger group, to widen our capacity for discernment and our agency. This is, perhaps, what Charlemagne, who was King of the Franks from 768, of the Lombards from 774, and of the Romans from 800, and who united Western and Central Europe, had in mind when he said that "to have another language is to possess a second soul." It is also the meaning of the Chinese proverb: "To learn a language is to have one more window from which to look at the world."

Learning a second language is, of course, more than learning how similar meanings can be conveyed by different symbols and sounds; it is about more than the ability of translating one set of linguistic codes into another. A language provides access to another culture, to different ways to experience the world and make meaning of it. Ludwig Wittgenstein, the philosopher, expressed this idea as follows: "If we spoke a different language, we would perceive a somewhat different world," and the Persian poet Rumi said it in these words: "Speak a new language so that the world will be a new world." That is also the meaning of the Turkish proverb: "One who speaks only one language is one person, but one who speaks two languages is two people."

The access to the different visions of life which multiple languages offer considerably expands our capacity for discernment and our agency. It helps us not just to understand others but to understand ourselves with depth and with perspective. It *decenters* us from the egocentrism and parochialism that result from living within a single linguistic community. Monolinguals are like fish in the water of their own language, a water they can't really see or understand. The great writer of the Enlightenment Wolfgang von Goethe said of learning foreign languages that "Those who know nothing of foreign languages know nothing of their own."

It is in this capacity of the learning of a foreign language to expand our view of ourselves and others, and to understand how our own linguistic community shapes us, that foreign languages relate to the development of global citizens.

In this highly readable and practical book, Erin Austin explains how foreign language instruction and global education reinforce each other. Drawing on her own experience as a foreign language teacher and on her studies of the subject, Erin examines multiple pathways to help students learn foreign languages and become global citizens. From travel abroad, to hosting a foreign student, from projects to learn about the Sustainable Development Goals to projects that engage students remotely with peers in other countries, this book offers a rich selection of options for foreign language teachers to help their students expand their discernment and their agency to *gain a second soul*. I especially enjoyed Erin's discussion of learning a foreign language as a multidimensional process, involving knowledge, as well as emotions and behaviors. A second language, when deeply learned, provides indeed access to the emotional lives of our interlocutors; it allows us to see not just with our eyes but with our hearts. In the eyes of Antoine de Saint Exupéry in the beautiful story *Le Petit Prince*: "On ne voit bien qu'avec le coeur. L'essentiel est invisible pour les yeux."

I met Erin when she was awarded a coveted fellowship as a teacher leader by the National Education Association Foundation. As part of the leadership development program, the fellows participated in a retreat in which I engaged them in dialogue about global citizenship education. I invited her and her colleagues to collaborate in the development of curriculum aligned with the United Nations' Sustainable Development Goals. The purpose of the activity was to support these teacher leaders in discovering the power of collaborative work to make education more relevant for their students, aligning their instruction with the ambitious and inclusive vision represented by the United Nations' Sustainable Development Goals. It was also the goal of the activity to engage the participants in the fellowship in an activity where they would see their leadership expanded as a result of developing professional knowledge, relevant to supporting professional practice. Over the course of a year, this group of teacher leaders collaborated across all states in the United States, using digital technologies, in the development and evaluation of a prototype of a curriculum to educate global citizens, which was published as a book in hopes that this type of collaborative work would inspire others in the profession.

Reading Erin's book on the subject of educating global citizens in the foreign language classroom gives me great pleasure. It is the kind of intellectual work that can support the improvement of professional practice. It also exemplifies the type of contribution that teachers can make to advance the profession, as they draw insights from and theorize their practice, and make this knowledge accessible to others in the profession.

I hope many teachers will read this book as I think they, and most importantly their students, would draw benefit from it. It offers good insights and a roadmap to educate students so they expand their discernment and their agency, but especially so they can find their shared humanity in others, across languages, and so they learn to see others not just with their eyes but with their hearts.

Learning Foreign Languages in Order to See with Our Hearts
By Fernando M. Reimers
Ford Foundation Professor of the Practice of International Education
Harvard Graduate School of Education

Preface

All teachers remember that moment when a certain spark was ignited, the moment when a switch was flipped and something inside them called out, "Whoa. This is IT. This is what I have to do." For many world language teachers, that moment happened while traveling.

In March of 1999, I took my first trip to Paris, and that's when it hit *me*.

In January of that year, I was a teaching assistant, for college credit, during January term of my college's 4-1-4 calendar. I was fortunate enough to be assisting Lisa Showers and her middle school French classes. Lisa had been my most influential teacher growing up, and she had a remarkably special flair—a certain *je ne sais quoi*—that is simply intangible. I was thrilled to be back in my hometown and learning from her; specifically, I was eager to see the teacher side of things. I wanted to know what actually went into the way that she taught, related to kids, and understood the material.

During the month I assisted her, we talked endlessly about Paris, and Lisa learned that I had never been there. One day, she was practically jumping up and down she was so excited because she had just found round-trip tickets to Paris for $240. (You may be wondering, "How did people find airfare deals in 1999?" I had to think long and hard about it, but I think—I *think*—there was a section in the newspaper with travel deals and phone numbers to call to book them.)

As fate would have it, we had the same spring break, so on a whim, we booked the tickets for a trip together. I spent the next two months over the moon excited for what I was sure was going to be the best trip of my life.

The week before departure, the excitement was mounting. I was on cloud 9! I was beaming from ear to ear, 24–7! Nothing could bring me down!

Then my boyfriend dumped me…because he didn't get into Harvard. (In case it's not abundantly clear, I was not on the admission team.)

And just like that, my joy completely deflated. How could I possibly go to *Paris*, the City of *Love*, freshly *dumped*? That sounded positively torturous. On the other hand, putting an Atlantic-sized distance between me and Harvard's freshest reject seemed a good place to start. I was nervous about how this was going to pan out, but I decided to take my chances with the historically amorous French. A couple days later, I got on the plane.

I will never forget that first trip to Paris. I was an art major who stood before priceless works of art I had only studied in books and in dark lecture halls. I was a goody-two-shoes who felt sneaky drinking wine in hotel bathroom glasses, poured from a bottle in a paper bag, while sitting under the Eiffel Tower. I was a music lover who got locked in Père Lachaise Cemetery at closing time after visiting Jim Morrison's grave. (Not my finest moment.) And I was a French major who finally got to speak the language I was learning and loving with native speakers in a fully immersed environment. It was like the mother ship had called me home.

Everything in that city was—and still is—magical to me. It took just those few days for me to think, "Boyfriend, schmoyfriend! I have a new love: Paris!" Granted, seeing what seemed like an entire city making out around every turn wasn't the most fun, given my circumstances, but in retrospect, that prepared me for what I would encounter in the hallways as a future high school teacher. It was a sort of professional development, if you will.

This is all to say that that trip to Paris *changed me*. It opened up an entirely new world and culture, and it fueled my desire to continue learning the language, make connections, and, most importantly, explore the world.

I am confident that every world language teacher has a similar story, a parallel tale with a country, a city, or a culture that ignited a spark in deep inside *them*. For some, like me, it's a trip to a far-off, seemingly mystical and magical land. For others, it may or may not have involved travel, but there was certainly a turning point: a point at which the country, heritage, and language you were born into took on a new meaning (Figure 0.1).

What was it for *you*? What ignited the spark?

Was it a first experience in a place that will forever hold a piece of your heart? If so, what is the place that inspired you to stand up in front of students and teach the language spoken there? What is the place that, year after year, when you talk about it with students, you absolutely come alive? Who were the people you experienced that location with, and what did you see? What *stuck* from that first adventure and why?

Or, conversely, what was the turning point with an already-familiar place for you? Was there an experience you had with your family that created a mindset shift? Was it something a family member said or a story someone told that made you look at your heritage differently? If you teach the language of your heritage, what made the language transform from "something you speak" to "something you *feel* and that you are driven to *share*"?

FIGURE 0.1 First trip to Paris, March of 1999 (me on the right)

I invite you to keep those feelings at the forefront as you read this book. Let them be your guide as you consider ways to deliver similarly transformative opportunities for kids.

It is these feelings that are the foundation of my desire to create global experiences for all kids. Throughout my years of learning about the global education movement, time and time again, I keep coming back to that spark I had and wondering, "How can I create environments in which a spark can ignite?" I don't get it right every time, I can't do everything at once, and I don't have unlimited funds. But I keep my eye on the prize: forward movement.

Taking small steps that, over time, lead to meaningful, lasting growth in students' hearts and minds—growth that will improve the world—is what this book is all about. My aim is to provide you with ideas, strategies, and resources to support you along the way. The first step in this journey is establishing an understanding of global education.

SECTION 1
The Case for a Global Connection Plan

1
Understanding Global Education

When I first began my journey with global education, I mistakenly—and very arrogantly—assumed I was already doing it, simply by virtue of being a world language teacher. "I teach a language that is spoken on five continents, and I teach cultural info from where the language is spoken. Clearly, that's global education, right?" I thought.

Wrong.

Most glaringly, although a world language *plays a role in* global education, it is not all-encompassing, nor anywhere near it. Second, what was I teaching? French. Where was the "cultural information" I was teaching originating? France. Whose stories and culture was I centering in my classroom? The French. And who are the French? According to World Atlas, France is approximately 85% white and 63–66% Christian (largely nonpracticing Catholics).

On the one hand, France has held the top spot of world tourist destinations for more years than I can count, and throughout my life, I have yet to meet someone who does *not* want to go to Paris in their lifetime. It can also be argued that France is the "mothership" of the language I teach. But France itself is not representative of the entire francophone world, a world that spans five continents. Not even close. Approximately 70% of the global francophone population are African (World Atlas).

It's all there in the name: *global* education. This approach spans borders, continents, and cultures. But what does that look like in our classrooms?

Defining a Movement

Global education isn't learning <u>about</u> the world; it is learning <u>with</u> and <u>from</u> the world.

When I first heard that statement, sitting in a hotel conference room in Washington DC, my professional world was rocked. That was the exact phrase that made me realize how wrong— or, rather, woefully incomplete—my thinking was that simply by teaching a world language I was using a global education model.

World language teachers can be quite skilled at teaching *about* the world; it's at the core of our classes. But when I truly consider how many world language classrooms I've ever known of or been a part of that consistently uphold the practice of learning *with* and *from* the world, the answer is astoundingly few.

So how do we make the leap from learning *about* the world to learning *with* and *from* the world? What defines that shift?

Centering Global Competence

Global education aims to create young people who are globally competent, empathetic citizens who actively engage in the world for the betterment of humanity. Increasing global competence is at the very heart of global education. Let's first take a look at two definitions:

Global competence is the disposition and capacity to understand and act on issues of global significance.

This definition is used by both World Savvy and the Asia Society's Center for Global Education, two powerhouses in the field of global education. In her 2014 TEDx Talk, Dana Mortenson, the founder of World Savvy, transformed her definition and said this:

Global competence is the ability to equip all students with the knowledge, the skills, and the dispositions to thrive in an interconnected and interdependent global society.

As so many language teachers do, you may be reading those definitions and picking out key words. Like me, you may even group key words by their parts of speech. Those words have a remarkable amount of power. For example, the latter definition calls us not just to *teach* students certain knowledge, skills, and dispositions, but rather to *equip* our students with those nouns. To me, that's a significantly more exciting verb!

When we analyze the definitions (a world language teacher super power), we can see that both the words themselves and how they land in us can be grouped into three main categories: social-emotional, behavioral, and cognitive. Table 1.1 starts the conversation of what we might expect to see in a world language class in each of those categories.

TABLE 1.1 Key Dimensions and Characteristics of Global Competence

Emotional Globally Competent Students Are:	**Behavioral Globally Competent Students:**	Cognitive Globally Competent Students:
◆ Empathetic. ◆ Open. ◆ Curious. ◆ Creative. ◆ Concerned. ◆ Eager. ◆ Generous. ◆ Collaborative. ◆ Humanitarian.	◆ Are involved inside and outside the school. ◆ Collaborate with diverse groups. ◆ Travel. ◆ Participate in acts of service. ◆ Explore. ◆ Read from diverse sources.	◆ Think critically. ◆ Are geographically aware. ◆ Are bilingual or multilingual. ◆ Engage in problem-solving more than complaining. ◆ Draw connections between languages. ◆ Draw connections between world language class content and that of other disciplines.

If you are thinking that some of the behaviors, in particular, in Table 1.1 are largely dependent on family situation, you're absolutely right. It can be difficult, if not impossible, for students who have to work every day after school to help support their family to be heavily involved in sports and activities the school offers. Similarly, families who are currently living in poverty will likely not have the means to travel far. While these statements are often true, it is also true that behaviors such as being involved in and out of school and traveling are not limited by a binary view. It's not a question of either you can do it or you can't; it's a question of scheduling. PK-12 and university systems need to analyze when opportunities for involvement on their campuses are offered to ensure greater equity. It's also wise to consider how we can embed activities into the school day. Activities like clubs may be able to meet during lunchtime, and service learning could be integrated into any class period. Likewise, when we think of travel, it's from a privileged place that our minds go directly to traveling abroad. Traveling outside of one's neighborhood, for example, can offer incredible benefits and, depending on where you live, can expose a person to rich diversity of language, ethnic background, religion, and culture.

It is worth noting that there are some who prefer the term "global readiness" to "global competence," arguing that we shouldn't aspire to something as comparatively low as simple "competence." Currently, global competence is the term most widely used in education, and global readiness is more commonly found in business circles. Despite agreeing with the criticism, for the purposes of this book, I will use the term "global competence" in order to align with colleagues in education.

World Savvy

Dana Mortenson and Madiha Murshed founded World Savvy in 2002 with the mission of educating and engaging youth to learn, work, and thrive as responsible global citizens. Mortenson and Murshed rightly noted that the American public school system was established with the intent to educate students for "standardized jobs in homogenous communities." The latest technological revolution has massively transformed jobs, business, and the way the world interacts, but the structure of the school system has not yet experienced the same level of transformation. As a result, businesses have become increasingly vocal about PK-12 schools not educating for what the workforce actually needs.

In her November 2015 article in *Education Week*, "What Do We Mean When We Talk About Global Education," author Homa Sabet Tavangar, notes

> According to a major IBM survey of more than 1,500 chief executive officers from 60 countries and 33 industries worldwide, chief executives believe that 'more than rigor, management discipline, integrity, or even vision—*successfully navigating an increasing complex world will require creativity*'.

She goes on to note that "This requires qualities like collaboration, entrepreneurial thinking (being alert to possibilities so that you can address them using creativity), empathy, and deeper problem-solving—in short, a global mindset."

As a public school teacher, it can be difficult and discouraging to hear that we're not doing enough and that we're not educating students for what the world needs them to know. But we have a choice: We can be part of the status quo or part of a transformative solution. And as we know, if we don't take the lead, a policymaker will take the lead for us, and they won't know what we know about educating students.

Stepping up to challenges can be wildly invigorating, and I believe world language teachers are poised to be the leaders in this work. We have excitement and passion toward teaching students about the world. The challenge is to integrate modern students *into the world*, for it's no longer appropriate (was it ever?) to treat learning about the world the same way as we treat a visit to the zoo or art museum. It's outdated to see students as visitors and the rest of the world as "exhibits" that they learn about and observe through a barrier; there's no interaction, and at the end of the day, we pull away from the parking lot and go home. That model establishes (for young students) and reinforces (for older students) the idea of the "other." We can look, we can learn, we can enjoy, and we can find immense beauty, but ultimately, we're separate, and we don't share the world. Technological advances in communication, travel, and industry no longer hold us separate, and our educational experiences should evolve to reflect the same oneness.

Just as Rome wasn't built in a day, neither is a global mindset nor global competence. Figure 1.1 is World Savvy's Global Competence Matrix, their guide to transformation in our classrooms.

The Core Concepts aspect of the matrix outlines, in my view, what those doing the work of global education believe. These are the "why" statements, if you will—the backbone along which global competence is rooted. Because we believe X, we are going to put in the work of integrating Behaviors, modeling Values & Attitudes, and cultivating global Skills in our learners.

In the Behaviors piece of the puzzle, I see elements drawn from different disciplines. For example, "Forms opinions based on exploration and evidence" is intimately tied to the scientific method used in a variety of science classes. "Adopts shared responsibility and takes cooperative action" could be taken right out of the playbook (pun intended) of a coach of a team sport or a physical education teacher. "Shares knowledge and encourages discourse" could come from a Speech & Debate class description or syllabus. The key is seeing that what different disciplines value benefits all learners and can be modified and used throughout a well-rounded, globally-centered curriculum.

Each of the Values & Attitudes, to me, adds up to two central themes. The first is constant growth. Woven throughout this list is both the triumph of learning and the knowledge that what we know can always be challenged and then broken down, reinforced, or added onto. The idea of learning being continuous helps to dismantle the disease of perfectionism as well because "perfect" implies an endpoint—*I'm done! It's perfect!*—but continual learning doesn't allow the learner to stop because there is no "I've arrived!" to be had.

Understanding Global Education ♦ 9

The second theme I see is humanizing education. Paul Emmerich France's work in personalizing and humanizing education gets to the heart of these principles. France says, "We must

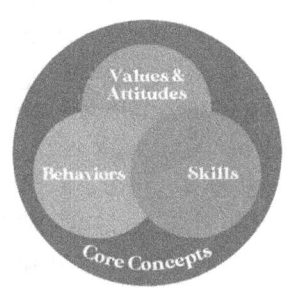

The Global Competence Matrix

Global competence is the disposition and capacity to understand and act on issues of global significance. Globally competent individuals possess and apply the following qualities, characteristics, and abilities to learn about and engage with the world. Educators who aspire to help students become globally competent must both develop these attributes in themselves and find ways to foster them in students.

Values & Attitudes

- Embraces new opportunities, ideas and ways of thinking
- Engages willingly and openly with others
- Demonstrates self-awareness about identity and culture, and sensitivity and respect for differences
- Values multiple perspectives
- Finds comfort with ambiguity and unfamiliar situations
- Reflects on the context and meaning of our lives in relationship to something bigger
- Questions prevailing assumptions
- Adapts to new situations and is cognitively nimble
- Chooses empathy
- Demonstrates humility

Core Concepts

- World events and global issues are complex and interdependent
- One's own culture and history is key to understanding one's relationship to others
- Multiple conditions fundamentally affect diverse global forces, events, conditions, and issues
- The current world system is shaped by historical forces

Behaviors

- Seeks out and applies an understanding of different perspectives to problem solving and decision making
- Forms opinions based on exploration and evidence
- Commits to the process of continuous learning and reflection
- Adopts shared responsibility and takes cooperative action
- Shares knowledge and encourages discourse
- Translates ideas, concerns, and findings into appropriate and responsible individual or collaborative actions to improve conditions
- Approaches thinking and problem solving collaboratively

Skills

- Investigates the world by framing questions, analyzing and synthesizing relevant evidence, and drawing reasonable conclusions that lead to further enquiry
- Recognizes, articulates, and applies an understanding of different perspectives (including their own)
- Selects and applies appropriate tools and strategies to communicate and collaborate effectively
- Listens actively and engages in inclusive dialogue
- Is fluent in 21st century digital technology
- Demonstrates resiliency in new situations
- Applies critical, comparative, and creative thinking and problem solving

www.worldsavvy.org

FIGURE 1.1 World Savvy's Global Competence Matrix

teach and learn in the pursuit of a deeper sense of collective humanity—and for no other reason." Our collective humanity is borderless. Instead, let's strive to be bound by empathy, curiosity, and cross-cultural engagement.

The Skills quadrant of World Savvy's matrix is a combination of both hard and soft skills. For example, being "fluent in 21st century digital technology" is a hard skill, or more often, a *set* of hard skills, but "listening actively" is a soft skill. It's increasingly apparent that employers need workers that are fluent in both hard and soft skills, but it's often only the hard skills that are taught explicitly. It is to students' benefit that the soft skills are taught explicitly as well. Weaving these skills into our curriculum in an implicit way is helpful, but it doesn't reach all learners. Explicit instruction in skills, combined with modeling by the teacher, can lead to more lasting results.

The Asia Society

The stated purpose of the Asia Society is "to navigate shared futures for Asia and the world across policy, arts and culture, education, sustainability, business, and technology," and their educational arm is the Center for Global Education (CGE). The CGE has a mission "to develop global competence in students, young leaders, and educators as the foundation for understanding between people in the U.S., the Asia Pacific region, and throughout the world."

Importantly, the CGE stresses the idea of global *leadership*—developing capacities, across disciplines, to lead progress and growth across the globe—and it has developed performance outcomes, rubrics, and "I Can" statements to support their work for kindergarten through postsecondary classrooms. These resources are free and downloadable from their website and work in concert with their Four Domains of Global Competence (Figure 1.2).

These domains—Investigate the World, Recognize Perspectives, Communicate Ideas, and Take Action—offer a baseline for what we can do in our classrooms. The real work comes in when we consider

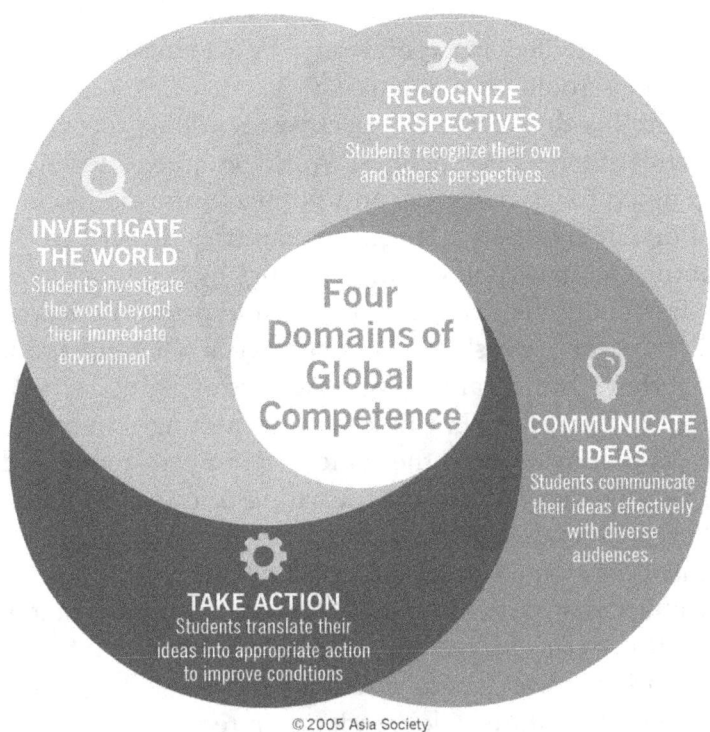

FIGURE 1.2 The Asia Society's Four Domains of Global Competence

how we can integrate the concept of learning with and from the world into each component.

Component 1 is Investigate the World: Students investigate the world beyond their immediate environment. The key word is *investigate*, which requires deeper action and thought. Traditionally, in a world language classroom, we investigate the world from that "outside looking in" perspective. We learn about the culture, customs, language, and geography of the locales in which our target language is spoken. Often, this is limited to focusing largely on one country. Global education requires higher order thinking and deeper dives into issues of global significance. For example, we may teach food and restaurant vocabulary along with cultural culinary norms of a country, but how would it impact students' global view if we also taught the larger concept of food shortage in our target language countries or regions? What if we investigated the causes of food shortage and wrote and/or spoke about possible solutions? Or if we invited an expert from a target language country to visit our classroom via a video chat?

Component 2 is Recognize Perspectives: Students recognize their own and others' perspectives. World language teachers often integrate cultural, religious, and political information, for example, of one or two target language countries. It's critical to be aware of the countries and cultures we highlight in our classrooms. For French teachers, it's easy to slip into primarily teaching about France; for Spanish teachers, primarily teaching about Mexico. As author Chimamanda Ngozi Adichie explained so eloquently about in her 2009 TED Talk, there is a danger in single story. It is vital that we expand the content of our classroom, and to do that, yes, we need to do some learning of our own (more ideas for that in Chapter 23).

Component 3 is Communicate Ideas: Students communicate their ideas effectively with diverse audiences. Communication, generally, we think of as "easy" and naturally embedded into our classrooms. *Teaching students to communicate in the target language is what I do every day!* we think. Global education requires us to take those communication skills and act on them outside of our classroom. It's the "diverse audiences" part of the equation that we often miss, yet it doesn't need to be a massive shift. There is a trend for the integration of what some call "glocality," or the idea that "global is local." How can we get our students communicating outside of the classroom (near and far) and, the flip side of the same coin, how can we bring diverse audiences *in* to communicate with our students?

Component 4 is Take Action: Students translate their ideas into appropriate actions to improve conditions. In the past, we may have raised money to send to a cause in a country that speaks our target language. I am not arguing that this is not valuable; however, I do argue that it's incomplete. One-directional work contributes to the "us versus them" dichotomy, and it can easily be felt and seen as "WE are helping YOU" (i.e., a "savior" mentality). The goal is to move it progressively toward a "Let's work together because my humanity is tied to yours" approach. With the possibilities modern technology offers, students can—and should—collaborate and innovate with peers around the world.

We have the means to make the "action" piece of the puzzle more two-directional that it has ever been.

More than likely, one of the thoughts going through your mind when hearing ways to stretch the four components from what we have traditionally done into ways to make it more global is, "But how do I do that in the target language?" This is a fair question. Staying 80–90% in the target language during each class, as well as making the language that we use comprehensible to students, is undeniably important, and I don't deny that. It is the way to acquisition and, ultimately, fluency.

I am curious if most world language teachers would argue that our classes are meant to have a singular focus, however. Is our sole goal language acquisition? Is that the only outcome we value? Each level of language is different, as are the students at each level, but if we have goals *in addition to* language acquisition, I see little wrong with supporting those goals in the best way we know how...including if that means using the students' primary language. I'm not advocating that we teach outside of our target language all period, every period. But if we teach part of a lesson in English in order to teach a concept that is critical for gaining global competence, yet the rest of the week we can keep a high percentage of target language use, our overall percentage of target language use is *still high*. We are tasked with creating bilingual (or multilingual) students, but if we cut off one of their languages completely, we are cutting off one of their skills as opposed to facilitating its growth.

The United Nations' Sustainable Development Goals (SDGs)

The SDGs are an inextricable component of global education. They were adopted by UN member states in 2015, and they can easily provide an interdisciplinary way of delivering content. The 17 goals are as follows:

1. No Poverty: End poverty in all its forms, everywhere.
2. Zero Hunger: End hunger, achieve food security and improved nutrition, and promote sustainable agriculture.

3. Good Health and Well-Being: Ensure healthy lives, and promote well-being for all at all ages.
4. Quality Education: Ensure inclusive and equitable, quality education, and promote lifelong learning opportunities for all.
5. Gender Equality: Achieve gender equality, and empower all women and girls.
6. Clean Water and Sanitation: Ensure availability and sustainable management of water and sanitation for all.
7. Affordable and Clean Energy: Ensure access to affordable, reliable, sustainable, and modern energy for all.
8. Decent Work and Economic Growth: Promote sustained, inclusive, and sustainable economic growth, full and productive employment, and decent work for all.
9. Industry, Innovation, and Infrastructure: Build resilient infrastructure, promote inclusive and sustainable industrialization, and foster innovation.
10. Reduced Inequalities: Reduce inequality within and among countries.
11. Sustainable Cities and Communities: Make cities and human settlements inclusive, safe, resilient, and sustainable.
12. Responsible Production and Consumption: Ensure sustainable production and consumption patterns.
13. Climate Action: Take urgent action to combat climate change and its impacts.
14. Life Below Water: Conserve and sustainably use the oceans, seas, and marine resources for sustainable development.
15. Life on Land: Protect, restore, and promote sustainable use of terrestrial ecosystems, sustainably manage forests, combat desertification, halt and reverse land degradation, and halt biodiversity loss.
16. Peace, Justice, and Strong Institutions: Promote peaceful and inclusive societies for sustainable development, provide access to justice for all, and build effective, accountable, and inclusive institutions at all levels.
17. Partnerships for the Goals: Strengthen the means of implementation, and revitalize the global partnership for sustainable development.

Every subject, including world language, can integrate the SDGs into planning and delivery of content, though not every content area needs to tackle every SDG for students to gain a firm understanding. Ideally, it's a team effort, and if an entire department or institution takes on the SDGs as an overarching theme, students will finish their studies there with more knowledge on the SDGs than most adults have. Chapter 15 takes a deeper dive into what that can look like in a world language classroom.

A Global Mindset Bound by Empathy

Homa Sabet Tavangar notes, "Practicing humility, empathy, and deliberate reflection doesn't come automatically with a passport," and nor do those qualities come automatically with a world language class. She goes on to say that a global mindset requires four main aspects: collaboration, entrepreneurial thinking, empathy, and deeper problem solving.

We have to be intentional about creating an environment and offering learning experiences that cultivate the qualities we hope to see in globally competent students. This doesn't require world language teachers to change our entire curriculum. It does, however, require us to consider our learning goals, our delivery, and the evolution of our classroom from one that is based on producing industrial workers to one that prepares students for a modern world. The world that students will experience after leaving our institutions is nothing if not interconnected and interdependent.

That interconnected and interdependent world, if it is to function peacefully for the prosperity of all, relies on empathy as a guiding force. In his work at the Harvard Graduate School of Education, Dr. Fernando Reimers stresses empathy as a central tenant of global education, saying, "To be fully human, we have to connect and empathize with every other human." Beautiful…and a tall order, certainly in the wake of atrocities such as war, injustices, and inequalities of all kinds. But it's worth working toward. It's worth putting in the effort to move the needle during our time on this earth.

Why Global Education?

I believe it's past time to modernize our educational system. As Richard Riley said, "We are preparing students for jobs that do not yet exist, using technologies that haven't been invented, to solve problems we have never heard of." There is simply no way we can do that using only the tools and structures of the past. Educational leaders at all levels are called to take the best of what we have always used, modernize it, and then build forward. We also need the humility to let go of stagnant structures, resources, and even lessons that we love but that no longer prepare students for the future. Stagnation may be comfortable, but it doesn't create excellence in our own work nor in the development of our students' minds and hearts.

I also believe what Gordon Brown, former U.K. prime minister, said in his 2009 TED Talk, *Wiring a Web for Global Good*: "The power of our moral sense allied to the power of modern communications and our ability to organize internationally...that, in my view, gives us the first opportunity as a community to fundamentally change the world." The key word there is *community*, but as a Brit, he's not talking about the London community or the UK community; he's talking about the global community. There's power in understanding that we are one. We are no longer separate, and we're increasingly becoming more globalized. Brown argued that modern communication will lead to a heightened global view with greater connectedness and empathy. And what is it that we do in our classes if not teach students how to communicate? World language teachers are better equipped to lead the development of global communication goals and advancement better than anyone else in education. We are experts in communication, and we have the fantastic opportunity to lead in a global manner and on a worldwide stage.

Global education is the perfect fit for decolonization efforts of our world language curriculum. Almost by definition—*learning with and from the world*—global education holds a decolonized, anti-colonial curriculum as a central aim. With a global education-based approach, the barriers and borders that formerly caused students (and teachers) to see speakers of our target language as the "other" fade away. Brilliantly, teachers are no longer charged with knowing (or feeling like we need to know) everything about every country where our target language is spoken. Instead, we rely more heavily on expert teachers and students from around the globe. Global education teaches students that "community" isn't limited to their classroom. Increasingly, students recognize peers and teachers throughout the world as part of their community. In doing so, the colonial view is attacked, and the single narrative becomes obsolete.

Lastly, global challenges require global solutions. We cannot tackle climate change or famine, for example, with a country-by-country approach. The same can be said of health, racial, income, and gender equality as well. The way forward is not in 195 separate plans, but it is in a global approach. We cannot expect adults in positions of power to know how to do this simply by virtue of age. That has not proven effective, and it is not an active approach; it's a default approach that is weak, at best, and a catastrophic failure at worst. That is why we need to start at the youngest levels of education. As soon as students enter the school systems, worldwide, they need to make age-appropriate connections with the rest of the world. If students grow up in a spirit of global collaboration, and in a spirit of interdependence and global friendship, the world can be changed for the good at a faster rate than we've ever seen in human history.

We have the means and the capacity to do this work, and I believe it's a moral imperative that educators make a commitment to dive in. World language educators, specifically, are poised to lead.

The First Step

World Savvy and the Asia Society are major players and leaders in the field of global education. The United Nations' SDGs and the trait of empathy are also inextricably linked to the work. But how, then, do we sift through it all? How do we decide where our focus can or should lie? Is there one matrix that is "better" than the other?

As you read through the ideas, strategies, and resources to promote global competence in Sections 2 and 3, keep in mind the basic notion that global education is *teaching and learning with and from the world*. The matrixes, the SDGs, and the key vocabulary wound throughout are all in service to that statement. We then have the power to choose how to best implement the principles for our students and with our specific knowledge and educational expertise.

Raising and educating globally competent citizens undoubtedly improves our world, but that may feel unreasonably ambitious for some teachers. *Wow? I thought I just had to teach Japanese. Now I'm tasked with <u>making the world better</u>?*

It boils down to this: Ignite the spark, and give students credit. We are not responsible for the full formation of a globally competent human, nor are we responsible for an entire classful of them. It's a team effort, to be sure. Strangely, we often leave out a key member of that team: the student. If we ignite the spark, the students, more often than we acknowledge, can take it from there.

2

Creating a Global Connection Plan

Once we have an idea of what global education is and why it's valuable, we can start sorting out how to implement it in our own context. This chapter is the story of how that started and evolved for me. It is my hope that it will give ideas for your own process, as well as show that the journey isn't a straight line, nor is it ever "finished."

Five years after my first trip to Paris, I was a young teacher leading my inaugural group of students to France. Although Paris was no longer brand new to me—I had been there multiple times by that point—I still experienced that same magic. This time, it was through the eyes of my students! I left wanting every student to have that "I've never done anything so *awesome!*" feeling.

Over the years, I've seen those expressions of joy again and again in my student travelers. However, I came to realize through my journey with global education that what I was providing wasn't adequate. Student travel, as much as I believe in its worth and power for transformation, doesn't reach enough kids; it privileges the few, not the many. The problem was that I didn't know how to fix it. I didn't know how to create the same spark I had experienced that first time in Paris for more than the dozen or so kids I would bring abroad every one to two years.

I determined that, largely, my vision was too narrow. I wasn't thinking creatively enough, and I wasn't paying attention to what excited students. I naïvely assumed that everyone's spark would be as uselessly poetic as mine: a sudden burst of uninhibited Parisian love...fueled by fumes from the tiny bottles of Jack Daniel's that many a hippie left to adorn Jim Morrison's gravesite...aided by a visceral emotional reaction from being in room of Impressionist masterworks...all wrapped up in the seductive smell of baguettes wafting out of boulangeries in the morning. For me, it was immediate and all-consuming, igniting all of my senses. It was, to be sure, completely over the top.

My students' sparks, however, could be all over the place. They might ignite while in my high school classroom and then be a slow burn for years after. Or maybe they could take a while to light in the first place. They might flicker on and off. Some students might have more natural "kindling" in their world, and some, undoubtedly, have less.

No two classes of mine have ever been the same, nor any two students. Therefore, igniting a spark—a love, a curiosity, a quest—with a global experience calls for a multifaceted approach.

When I finally sat down to sketch out a fledgling improvement plan, I started with my goals. What, exactly, was I trying to accomplish? Ultimately, I wanted to increase students' global competence. I wanted language skills to soar and, importantly, for students to have a reason to *want* to improve their language skills. I wanted them to create connections with and feel empathy toward people around the world. In establishing those connections, I hoped that students would maintain them and, after graduating, see no boundaries (literal or figurative) for where they could choose to live their lives, work, and put down roots. I envisioned some sort of peaceful utopia in which the young generation would be globally interconnected so much so that the thought of war would be a distant memory in history.

You know...change the world, right? No big deal.

Pulling myself back down to Earth, I got to work on goal setting. From here on, this chapter will walk you through parts of my process that demonstrate an evolution. You may feel a need to "get to the end result," and that's understandable. However—and this is likely because I work in an International Baccalaureate program where the process always trumps the end result—I do feel like peeling back the curtain can provide ideas, share insight, and create a more human feeling to this work.

I settled on four "ground-level" goals that I felt could feed those loftier goals down the road:

1. **Provide opportunities for students to interact on a global level. (Primary domains: Investigate the World, Recognize Perspectives)**

    I did, and still do, believe in the power of global travel to positively change the outlook, education, and lives of students. I can't conceive of a time in which that would change. But I also concede that that's *one* experience, and a pretty specific and costly one at that. I wondered if there were other ways that students could interact globally that would also create an impact. In short, I challenged myself to broaden my view.

    This is a goal over which I have control. I could quite easily make it into a SMART (specific, measurable, achievable, relevant, time-bound) goal: *By the end of semester 1, I will include one new global activity (insert the name of activity here) in levels 1 and 2.*

2. **Create opportunities for students to use their language skills with native speakers who live in other countries. (Primary domain: Communicate Ideas)**

    As a world language teacher, this was key. When students use their language with me, a non-native speaker, I'm sure it feels, in a way, false. They are deeply aware that I am American and that, like the majority of them, English is my first language. There's a safety net there. They know that despite the fact that I won't always answer them if they speak to me in English (depending on their level of French), they can *"Laissez tomber, Madame"* their way out of the situation and consult with someone else in order to get the answer in English. Historically, the majority (but certainly not all) of my students have been white and span the middle-class spectrum. Because of that shared background, without any research, they have a solid idea of my own culture, even if I never talked about my outside-of-school life at all. With native speakers, particularly those in other countries, the cultural safety net also disappears. Students are forced to use language in a different way, and the perceived knowledge of background is at least partially negated by the novelty of a (outwardly) different global culture.

Like goal #1, I have total control here. A SMART goal could be: *Over the summer, I will post on ePals for a partnership for the next school year with my level 1 class. By the end of September, I will have chosen and secured a partner classroom in another country, and by the end of October, we will have exchanged our first letters.*

3. **Increase students' global competence. (All four domains)**

In just three and a half years after I somehow booked that first flight to Paris without the benefit of Kayak or individual airline search features, I was a full-time teacher and suddenly working with students who would never know a world in which those tools *aren't* there. Since then, the speed at which technology has changed our day-to-day lives is dizzying, but it illustrates the point that the world I grew up in is not the world I am preparing my students for. At the tip of their fingers, my students can—and do—access music from across the world. They have social media connections that know no international boundaries. They have no sense, as a generation, that an eventual career needs to be located in the same geographic locale as one lives. Our students have a more open view than any generation in the history of what they can do for a living and where they can reside, and it is the job of teachers to help prepare them for success in an exciting world that some of us never grew up knowing. World language teachers are the professionals most equipped to do that because our expertise in language and culture can provide the support our students need to thrive in a global community as productive citizens, workers, and partners of all kinds.

Unlike goals #1 and #2, I do not have direct control over the outcome of this goal; I cannot make it into a SMART goal. Personally, I find it appropriate—and even desirable—to have different kinds of goals. You can think of them as SMART goals and outcome goals. In theory, the SMART goals will feed into the outcome goals and allow them to come to fruition. Nevertheless, it's important to note that outcome goals have their own pace, and that pace will be different for each student. Sometimes, we will not ever see that the goal was achieved because it happens after the student has left our context. We have to be okay with our part: laying the groundwork for the desired outcome to eventually happen when the right "ingredients" all come together for the student.

4. **Do #1–3 with an equity lens.**

Equity, for me, boils down to not necessarily giving every student the same things, but giving each student the tools that are appropriate for them and their unique needs.

If you're not yet well-versed in the term *equity*, allow me to use a sports analogy (and admittedly simplify). I grew up playing basketball, and I went to basketball camp almost every summer. Typically, there was a version of the same camp for different ages and genders of players. If the players at the camps were all treated *equally*, everyone would've received the exact same basketball and t-shirt. But the thought of giving a third grader a women's size large t-shirt and a men's basketball is laughable! What are they going to do with it? They'd drown in the t-shirt, and they're not strong enough to shoot a men's ball. They'd quickly become discouraged, and they wouldn't have fun. Similarly, what would a senior boy do with a kids' size ball and a youth small t-shirt? About all they could do is laugh. They couldn't wear the shirt, and a ball that is small wouldn't help them hone their skills on the court; it's not their "real world" as basketball players. Giving every camper/player the same "tools" is *equal*, but it's not *equitable*; it doesn't meet needs, and it doesn't support success. To be equitable, the camp organizers should give appropriate size balls and t-shirts and run drills that meet the skill levels of the campers.

Similarly, if I give every student the "opportunity" to go on a trip abroad with me, it's *equal*—"This trip is open to everyone!"—but it's not *equitable*. For some students, me saying that they have the option to pay thousands of dollars to miss one to two weeks of summer work time to gallivant across the globe is as useless to them as making a kindergartener shoot a basketball at a ten-foot rim. Equity in education raises the performance of all students and minimizes the gaps.

For this goal, like goals #1 and #2, teachers do have some amount of control. But like goal #3, this goal can happen at different paces for everyone. We are all at a different place in our understanding of equity and in building the tools that we have for implementing equitable practices; the key is to keep moving forward from our individual starting points.

Once my goals were laid out, my next step was to start with what I had. I knew I wasn't starting from zero, which was encouraging. I knew students had different learning needs. Some like being led, sitting back, and really taking in information before they're ready to take a deeper dive. Others are more of the "pass me the microphone and let me take charge" variety. I knew my students were coming to the classroom with different family backgrounds in a wide variety of ways. Not every student's family could afford a trip abroad, for example, and I needed to account for socioeconomic diversity. (Yes, there are other types of diversity that we encounter in our classrooms, but socioeconomic appeared to be the easiest to tackle from the start. Many of the other types of diversity—linguistic, cultural, neural, etc.—would be addressed as I progressed.) I also broadened my view of what "global" meant. It no longer was simply synonymous with "another country," like it was when I first started teaching. Instead, after studying global education, I knew it meant providing experiences that facilitated engagement outside of the school—a curricular reach that included a local, regional, national, and global scope.

And I needed a name for my fledgling project! What was it that I was creating? I was creating a framework to support global competence and create connections for students. I was a woman growing a *plan*. So there it was: my global connection plan. I liked "plan" better than "framework" because, in my experience, frameworks seem a little more fixed. Conversely, any plan I had ever been a part of or created left a lot of wiggle room for changing along the way.

With all of that in mind, I sketched out a simple box (Table 2.1).

I started filling in what I *already* had and what I *already* did. This included activities, resources, and experiences I offered. Looking at that first matrix I created, whoa—were there ever holes! Still, everyone starts somewhere. I asked myself if those activities and opportunities created globally competent students. Yes, they did, but there weren't enough of them. The reach wasn't there yet.

I asked myself if what I had on that original matrix was equitable. The answer there was a resounding, "Not at all!" I was supporting the few, not the many. I knew I could do better.

From there, I continually added to the global connection plan matrix. I implemented ideas that current and former colleagues use or had used, and I sought out new ideas, activities, and experiences. I also changed the wording from "students lead" to "student-intensive" and "students take in" to "adult-intensive." Version 2.0 (Table 2.2) felt better to me.

Over time—years, in fact—I added to the list inside each quadrant and the matrix as a whole into something I felt was substantial and much more equitable. I did not include each and every resource every year or in every level of French that I taught. Instead, it was a toolbox that I could go back to throughout the year and tweak depending on the students I had and what the school year itself looked like. The pandemic, for example, threw a real curveball to this work, but it also forced growth. That didn't always feel good in the moment—far from it!—but looking back, I'm grateful for the "COVID push."

TABLE 2.1 Global connection plan matrix ver. 1.0

Low-Cost, Students Lead	Low-Cost, Students Take In
High-Cost, Student Lead	High-Cost, Students Take In

TABLE 2.2 Global connection plan matrix ver. 2.0

Low-Cost/Student-Intensive	Low-Cost/Adult-Intensive
High-Cost/Student-Intensive	High-Cost/Adult-Intensive

Armed with a new, fuller, matrix, I started presenting this work at conferences, and I was encouraged by the interest I encountered. There was also a fantastic willingness for conference session attendees to share ideas, strategies, and resources with each other that they have used and found success with throughout their careers.

Despite forward momentum, I kept running into a problem. As I presented this work, explicitly chunking it into low-cost/student-intensive options, high-cost/student-intensive options, low-cost/adult-intensive options, and high-cost/adult-intensive options, I struggled with both language and meaning. Ultimately, I didn't feel like the words were right yet.

Language, as all world language teachers know, *matters*. Like so many of us, I am fascinated by language: its history, its use, and how to convey meaning with it. I kept getting stuck with the "student/adult-intensive" label, despite still thinking it was an improvement from the initial iteration that used "students lead" and "students take in." The problem I saw was that so many of the resources I was sharing (arguably, *all of them*) had countless methods of implementation, especially considering the variety of teachers and students who would use them. Something I saw as entirely student-driven another teacher might see best used as a teacher-driven activity, and vice versa. Even though I liked the look of a four-quadrant matrix, practicality and usefulness were more important than aesthetics, at least as far as the *base* of the plan is concerned.

The version of the global connection plan I use in this book is quite simple—divided only into low-cost (Section 2) and high-cost (Section 3) resources—though each part is full of opportunity and choices:

The chapters that follow are the work of fleshing out this plan, taking a hard look at each tool, and searching for ways in which I can do better for my students and, I hope, for yours too. The chapters in this book have three aims:

1. **To support world language teachers in understanding what global education is.**

    Hopefully, Chapter 1 laid the groundwork of your understanding. Global education is exciting and, I believe, the way forward for a world-class educational system.

2. **To support world language teachers with resources to create a global connection plan.**

    I introduce a variety of tools and ideas, and I invite you to consider how they could be modified to fit your students and context. I will share possibilities I see for the resources, and I encourage you to look at each possibility through your unique lens.
3. **To equitably give all world language students global experiences to prepare them for citizenship in a globalized world.**

    It is my hope that every reader will find something that can be used to enhance their classrooms, at whatever level they teach. Any sort of global shift, however (seemingly) small, supports students in living lives of global connectedness. At the most minimal level, a globally competent student has fun in a world they see as their playground, with global peoples they view as equals. But at the highest and most idealized level, the more we connect the world, the more we create a secure world. When the foreigner ceases to be foreign and instead is a friend or a partner of equal value and possibility, we contribute to peace, prosperity, and positive growth across the planet.

Before you get into the meat of these ideas, I have a few last thoughts that can be helpful as you navigate the content:

Each section of this book is designed to support teachers. Section 2 introduces a variety of resources, strategies, and ideas that cost little-to-no money to implement. Predictably, Section 3 introduces resources that are (at first glance) at the opposite end of the spectrum. Section 4 starts with supporting teachers in increasing their own global competence and then continues with support to keep your global education plan moving forward.

The Spotlight sections largely highlight public school teachers who are in the trenches, implementing these and related resources in creative ways, in a wide variety of American (U.S.) contexts. They share their experience, joys, successes, and pitfalls. Every one of us has ideas we have tried that have not worked, and I bet we all have things we look back on that we did in the past that we're no longer proud of because once we *knew* better, we *did* better. We can learn from failure or less-than-desired results, and I don't shy away from bringing it up. I also purposely include gender, age, linguistic, racial, and geographic variety in the stories, as well as including both retired and current teachers. Two Spotlights are from (now adult) former students who experienced the resources in the book, and some Spotlights feature school staff who are not in teaching roles but whose work and expertise can support world language teachers.

As you read about tools that support global readiness, some will jump out at you as being easy to immediately implement in your current context; conversely, others may not initially speak to you. This work doesn't have to be done isolation. In fact, it shouldn't be! This book isn't designed for one teacher to implement every strategy and use every resource presented within. Consider how your World Language department can create a *joint* global connection plan or, better yet, how this could expand from you, to your department, to your school, and to your whole PK-12 district or university setting. This is especially possible when we each challenge our view of what constitutes a global experience and maintain curiosity about would could be, both for ourselves and for our students.

It can be tempting to skip some or all of the resources under the "high-cost" umbrella, but there are reasons to reconsider that approach. First, life happens. There's no reason to assume that the teaching context we're currently in is going to look the same one year from now or five or more years from now. Change is inevitable. Policies may change. The student population may change. *We* might change—we could switch schools, student instructional levels, cities, or states. All of these changes bring new opportunities, and it's vital to have that toolbox handy. Second, and maybe this is a result of being the daughter of a frugal mother and a downright cheap grandfather, but I spend my day-to-day life looking for ways to make the expensive accessible…and I've become good at it. The chapters in Section 3 include ideas to bring the cost down so that the resources are more accessible to all students.

Finally, I invite you to sketch out your own global connection plan as you read. The plan here is simplified (low-cost, high-cost) because you will see different ways to rearrange the sections to fit your setting and create a fuller matrix. I caution you not to resort to a simple *list* because without sorting out the resources into at least two categories, it is too easy to overload in one area, resulting in a less equitable global connection plan. For you, it may be beneficial to sort out not only low- and high-cost resources but also low- and high-technology resources. Or it might be logical to sort based on what's appropriate for different ways of thinking and neurodiversity. Another approach is separating the resources into the categories of school, local, state, national, and international. You may find that the resources, to you, are very clear in being "student-intensive" or "adult-intensive," so one of my early versions of the matrix may work for you.

It may be compelling for you to arrange the experiences into language provided by World Savvy (Core Concepts, Behaviors, Values & Attitudes, Skills) or the Asia Society (Investigate the World, Recognize Perspectives, Communicate Ideas, Take Action). That's a fabulous idea! I don't, however, use those terms to group experiences in this book because, similar to the student-intensive versus teacher-intensive argument, 50 teachers will use a single resource in 50 different ways; there is no one "right" match for each resource, though I do offer my initial thoughts.

The point is that you create a structure to your global connection plan and matrix that works for you, for now, knowing that it will evolve over time…and being alright with (or even excited about!) that evolution.

SECTION 2
Leveraging Lower-Cost Options

3

Hosting

The most common global experience I have seen in world language education is offering student trips abroad. I have led trips for years, and I've loved it every time! There are scores of student travel opportunities available, and many include a host family stay. In my experience, these trips don't cost more money than trips that don't include in a family stay component.

I challenge world language professionals to pay more attention to the other—significantly less expensive—side of that travel coin: our students being the *hosts* instead of the *visitors*.

Establishing a hosting program provides a cultural exchange not just for the language student but for their entire family! (Two birds…) Unlike a trip abroad, students do not have to pay a fee to participate with a good, reputable program.

The goal is for the hosting student to share their life and that of their family with the visiting student. If your student is an only child, it is a chance to have a "sibling" for a short period of time. For families who are unable to travel for any number of reasons, it's a chance to experience (a piece of) the culture of another country right in their own home. Significantly, when a whole family experiences a visiting student in their home, the hearts and minds of more than just our student can be opened. Indeed, hosting impacts entire families.

There are numerous organizations that facilitate exchanges, and they all offer different program structures. The length of time for hosting can vary widely, as can the time of year. Often, families think of hosting in a traditional way: a visiting student in their home for a semester or a full school year. Those options certainly exist, but it can be a hard sell to families. *What if we don't like the visitor? What if they don't like us? What if it just doesn't work well?* Those fears are understandable. But it's a significantly easier sell to offer hosting programs that last one, two, or three weeks. This eases fears, and it is a more equitable option as well because more families are able to participate. Short-term options can be found during the school year as well as during the summer months. Sometimes, schools are not equipped to bring a visiting student in for short-term hosting (they're often better at semester or year-long options and have policies and procedures for such circumstances), so coordinating teachers and families may find it easier to choose a summer option.

Typically, the requirements for short-term hosting are simple:

1. Provide room and board (i.e., lodging and food) for your visiting student.
2. Provide the visiting student with their own bed. This can be a pullout couch or a standard bed. Students can share a room with a hosting family member, but they cannot share a bed.
3. Provide friendship by integrating the visiting student into your family life.

That's it! More often than not, hosting families will want to take the visitors on excursions and do activities with them, and although they aren't required to do anything out of the ordinary from what they typically do as a family, many *choose* to. It's helpful if the coordinating teacher gives families a list of ideas of what they can do, activity-wise, with their visitor. Table 3.1 provides an example of a handout that could be personalized to your region.

When discussing activities families can do with their visiting student, stress that visitors commonly find delight in things we would never think of as "fun." For example, a visitor

TABLE 3.1 Activity Ideas for Hosting Families

Little-to-No Cost	Low-to-Mid Cost	Special Treats/Day Trips
◆ A tour of the town ◆ Family movie night with popcorn (put on subtitles) ◆ Trip to the grocery store ◆ Trip to the bank ◆ Trip to the post office ◆ Trip to Target ◆ Make chocolate chip cookies as a family ◆ Make brownies as a family ◆ Family game night ◆ Hiking in your area ◆ Biking (see if you can borrow a bike from a friend for your host student) ◆ Exploring your downtown area ◆ Guest pass for your gym, if you belong to one ◆ Cook a big American breakfast (pancakes, waffles, French toast, eggs, bacon, sausage, orange juice—the host student has likely never had something like that!) ◆ Picnic in park ◆ Grill out (This is very American. If sweet corn is in season, your host student has probably never had it.) ◆ Fire with s'mores (so American!) ◆ A religious service (if the visitor is interested) ◆ Visit to a capital building ◆ Make "ants on a log" (peanut butter isn't common worldwide) ◆ Volunteer together	◆ Dinner at a restaurant (note: many European kids have likely *never* had Mexican food) ◆ Visit the mall ◆ Movie theater ◆ Dairy Queen (soft serve ice cream not common in all countries) ◆ Brunch (many visitors aren't used to the idea of brunch or of breakfast-only restaurants or menus) ◆ High school sporting event ◆ College sporting event ◆ Ice skating ◆ Check Groupon.com to find low-cost activities in the area ◆ Horseback riding ◆ An area arcade ◆ Summer water activities: paddle boarding, boating, fishing, mountain biking, local pool ◆ Winter snow activities: snowshoeing, cross-country skiing, sledding ◆ A high school, college, or community play ◆ An escape room ◆ Bowling ◆ Camping ◆ A museum visit	◆ Professional sporting event ◆ A concert ◆ A visit to a nearby city or touristy town ◆ Area attractions (e.g., zoo, amusement park) ◆ Visit another, nearby state

may enjoy seeing what it's like to go to the post office and mail a package. That's *new* to them! North American grocery store chains also offer experiences that students from many countries may never have encountered. *An entire aisle of just cereal? No way! I have to take a picture of this!* I still giggle every time a visiting student directly asks, "Can I see big yellow school buses? Do you really have them?" Students from other countries see American school buses as a cultural symbol that exists in movies, but that is never seen on their own streets. They are *thrilled* to see that they really do exist in the United States, and they often make a production out of taking photos of the school buses.

When families host during the summer, inevitably, parents are concerned about the family's summer schedule and how that can impact a visitor. *We work during the day. Is that a problem? My child has sport camp during the mornings of that first week the visitor will be here. Can we still host?* It's not an ideal time to host if the primary hosting student has an eight-hour job five days a week, for example, but if the idea is for a visitor to experience what life is like in another country, that includes understanding that family life is busy and has many working parts. As long as the visiting student isn't alone every day, a variety of family schedules can be accommodated.

So what do you, as a teacher, have to do to start a hosting program? Start with finding a good organization as your partner. A simple Google search is an efficient way to start. (Language & Friendship is my personal favorite for short-term exchanges.) Keep in mind what length of time is ideal for your context, as well as what time of year. After you find a few organizations that seem promising, reach out to each of them to determine if they facilitate exchanges in your area. Although exchanges happen in urban, suburban, and rural environments, access to an international airport in the general vicinity is usually key. Your chosen organization will have support for you, as well as a time frame of what should happen and by when. Often, they will provide dossiers of the visiting students ahead of time, and coordinating teachers can hand those out in class. Students quickly become excited reading about who is available to stay with them and what they enjoy doing. Students and families then reach out to the organization directly and submit an application. Some organizations pay the local teacher a stipend to do family visits and check references; others may have staff that complete those. Some organizations will work with local teachers (you or someone else) to be the primary contact for when the visitors are in their placements; often, this comes with a stipend too.

When the visiting students are in your area, you may or may not have an active role, depending on the structure of the organization you work with. Regardless, you, the world language teacher, are still the cultural expert, as far as the participating families are concerned. As such, it's helpful to provide the families some level of support, even if it's simply in the form of information. Tables 3.2 and 3.3 can be adapted into your own handouts for families who are preparing to host.

One of the most valuable outcomes from implementing a hosting program in your area is that, once again, the teacher may ignite the spark by *offering* a hosting opportunity, but we never know how far students will take it. Hosting has the potential to be the start of lifelong friendships. Don't be surprised if a student excitedly shares with you all the texts, photos, social media exchanges, and music recommendations from a student they hosted months or even years ago.

TABLE 3.2 Ideas for Welcoming Your Exchange Student

Welcoming an Exchange Student into Your Home

- Make a welcome sign for the airport, the front door, or the door to their room.
- As much as possible, try to eat as a family. (This is a great way for the visiting student to learn about families and customs.)
- Ask about their food preferences ahead of time, if possible.
- Make a small (and inexpensive) scrapbook or photo album of your family/town/school for the student to bring home with them when they leave.
- Initiate conversation by using open-ended questions instead of yes/no questions.
- Let the student know what your expectations are ("family guidelines").

TABLE 3.3 Tips for Communicating with Your Exchange Student

How Are We Going to Communicate?

The students coming to our area are highly motivated kids who have been studying English and are very interested in experiencing our national and regional culture. Your host sibling will speak with an accent and may have trouble, at times, expressing themselves in English. Please remember that English is a second language for them, and in many cases, a third or fourth language. There are several things you can do to better understand each other:

- Repeat what you have said in a different way if the student doesn't understand. Often, it is just a matter of vocabulary, not concept, that is difficult.
- Use dictionary apps.
- Use gestures to act out what you're trying to say. This can be fun!
- Although the visiting student is coming here to learn English, it can be helpful to use some of their first language with them as well. Better yet, ask them to teach you!
- Speak more slowly.
- Write things down. The North American and/or the specific regional accent may be difficult for some students to understand. It is not uncommon in other countries for students to be taught British English.
- Do not use slang…or, at least, don't <u>over use</u> it.
- Enunciate and speak clearly.

Equity in Hosting

In order to make hosting as equitable as possible—or, in other words, to increase the access to as many students as you can—first think about what kind of time frame and what time of year fits your context best. Often, short-term hosting programs (one to three weeks) can make it more accessible for families. It may be beneficial to survey families to find out what time of year (school year or summer holidays) is best; if they prefer summer, ask what month is best. But even then, you may receive a wide range of responses with no clear "right" answer. In that case, consider a cycle. Perhaps on odd years you offer a three-week hosting session in the summer, and even years you offer a one-week hosting session during the school year.

A fun, equitable outcome from hosting is that after a positive experience it is not uncommon for the visiting student's family to invite your student to travel to stay with them. This is an incentive for your students' families to create a welcoming and positive experience! A family may not be able to afford to send their student on a student trip you lead, but if all they have to come up with financially is the airfare, and their former visiting student's family will take care of the rest, travel suddenly becomes less of a dream and more of a real possibility for many.

As well as showing consideration to the time of year and length of the hosting period, consider the home countries of the visiting students. Let's use a French classroom as an example. France is not representative of the entire francophone world. To the extent possible, look for hosting organizations that facilitate exchanges with a variety of countries and contexts. One year, you might look to host students from an urban environment like Paris or Geneva, and the next year a smaller town in Belgium. Better yet, look for an organization that can add a francophone African or Caribbean group of students to the mix.

Tying Hosting to Global Education Principles

Hosting programs invite students—and families—to **Investigate the World** beyond their immediate environment by bringing the world to them. We should no longer hold the antiquated view that the "world" is, somehow, reserved to "out there." Hosting is a concrete way to bring "the world" into our own home.

Sharing everyday activities and cultural practices in the context of family supports **Recognizing Perspectives**. So much of those perspectives happen at the dinner table, sharing life as a family. The more students and parents pay attention to effective communication techniques, the more perspectives will be shared and discussed.

That same dinner table is effective in helping students **Communicate Ideas**. Ideas are communicated from the host family to the visitor and vice versa. Additionally, if the host student is then invited by the visiting student's family to spend time in their home, in their country, the whole process happens again. And let's not forget that students are social! It is rare that a visiting student spends their time exclusively with their host sibling. Commonly, the visiting student is introduced to a circle of friends, all of whom provide opportunities for communication and exchanging of ideas.

> **Educator Spotlight:** Cinthia Johnson
> **Position:** Spanish Teacher
> **School:** Amery High School
> **City, State:** Amery, WI
>
> **How did you get introduced to the idea/activity of your students hosting students from other countries in their homes?**
>
> I am a former exchange student myself, so since I was in school, I always wanted to travel to discover new cultures, customs, etc. When I started working at Amery High School, I had the opportunity to take students abroad to live the same experience as I did. I wanted my students to grow globally since there is a lot to learn around the world. Some of my students had their host siblings return to live with them as well. I bring my students abroad on trips that include family stays, and I also coordinate family stays in my local community.
>
> **What company do you use to facilitate the exchanges, and why do you like them?**
>
> I used Language & Friendship. What I like about them is that they allow students to connect with their host family months before the students go to their houses. The traveling students got to know their family, how they live, where they live, and be familiar with their activities.
>
> **What do you have to do, as a teacher, to get a hosting program running each year? How time-intensive is it?**
>
> As a teacher, I have to invite our former students to come to talk to the future travelers to talk about their experience and how this adventure changed their way of thinking or how to understand other cultures. Also, when my students travel to host families abroad, I had to make sure my students wrote a petition letter to the potential families and to prepare them with the language along with their mentality to see other things different to the ones they are used to. It is very

intensive because I want to make sure my students are prepared for any circumstances as much as possible. I put in many hours outside of school to prepare myself and my students, but in the end it is worth it.

When we had students from France and Argentina coming to the Amery community, they were placed by matching them with the family likes, gender, and ages. Each student had to write a letter to the future American host to introduce themselves and give more biographical information. The exchange student was able to be in contact with their families months before their arrival. They were able to be part of the school and be part of activities during their stay.

The process I did with my American students was the same for the foreign exchange students. The only difference is the American students just stayed with the family for no more than a week.

What are some tips you could give other teachers considering setting up a hosting program so that they can minimize potential problems either before or during hosting?

Always know there are a lot of ups and downs during the process. Not everything will run like it was planned. When my students were the travelers, I always was very direct with the students and had a contract with them. In this contract, you can write things like "You are expected to have excellent behavior in school as well as in their home." I recommend having monthly meetings to talk about the places they are going to stay and to learn about the town, people, food, economy, etc. When students from other countries come to Amery and are placed in host families here, I have weekly interviews with the foreign exchange student to check in.

What is some feedback you've had from students or families after they host?

The families so far have been very pleased with their students because they always were polite and wanted to learn more about the region or other places. They had an open mind about things that they never were exposed to before.

When my students were the exchange students, they expressed "In the beginning it was scary," even though they knew the family ahead of time, but as they started understanding the language more, their experience was fantastic. They expressed, "It was a life changing!"

How does hosting support increased global competence in students?

I think it makes a person vivid. They absorb the culture, the problems, and how citizens solve them according to their lifestyle and interests. Hosting allows them to be part of another society who fights for what they believe is correct for them. Like one of my student travelers said, "This experience lit my eyes to see how unlucky I was when I thought I lived in a country where everything is about money and power, instead of appreciating the value of the family and everything that surrounds it." In other words, they can see with the world issues with a better understanding.

4

World Language Storytime

My mother often recounts a tale of going to our local, public library when my sister and I were little. My sister had just had a birthday, and all she wanted now that she was a bona fide "big kid" was her own library card. When we got to the library, full of joy and excitement, we received the devastating news that my sister still had one year to go before she could have her own card. *Sobbing* ensued. I didn't blame her.

Libraries are magical. My sister wasn't the first child to cry upon learning she wasn't old enough to have her own library card, and she undoubtedly wasn't the last. Libraries provide access to magical worlds for anyone who picks up a book.

World language teachers would do well to tap into this literary magic and partner with local libraries. Librarians, by their very nature, it seems, are open to ideas that expand language and then capitalize on the joy of reading. The Poudre River District library system in Fort Collins, Colorado, created a free World Language Storytime program in several languages: French, Spanish, American Sign Language, Arabic, Russian, Mandarin, and Japanese. Their professionals created a fun, engaging structure, and there's no reason it can't be replicated anywhere in the world:

Hello song
Story #1

Movement/play-based interlude #1
Story #2
Movement/play-based interlude #2
Story #3
Goodbye song
Closing Craft

Storytime lasts about an hour, and the library provides a snack at the end. The entire event takes place in the target language (TL), and it is attended by a diverse group of people: children with families who speak the TL at home, children who are learning the TL in school, children whose families want to explore the TL, and parents and other adults who are simply interested in the TL.

This program provides older students or fluent adults the opportunity to interact and share. Advanced language students at the high school or university level are well suited to lead this or similar programming at your local library.

But my students aren't fluent speakers! Their language is accented! What if they make a mistake? These are fears that may arise. Consider, however, that just because someone is a native speaker doesn't mean their language is flawless. (For proof, simply take a look on social media!) Being a native speaker also doesn't mean we don't carry a regional accent in our first language. The fact that this type of activity does require a certain level of skill in the TL and that, yes, it may be more advanced, does not mean that it's not accessible. When we set the bar high, tell students we know they can reach it, and provide the right support for them to do so, it's remarkable what they can accomplish!

To support students, we can record ourselves (or a native speaker whose accent we prefer to our own) reading the stories the students will present and give the audio file to students. That way, they can work on the pronunciation when and where they choose. It's also a good idea that each student should be responsible for a *piece* of a story, not a whole story. This way of scaffolding the text is less overwhelming, and students can focus their efforts on a smaller chunk. Stronger students may be assigned (or may self-select into) a story with more difficult vocabulary and pronunciation, and more hesitant speakers may present a chunk with language they feel more comfortable with.

Storytime can be a cross-curricular project as well. Simply standing in front of young children and being the "older ones" in the room does not guarantee that the younger ones will listen. Toddlers and preschoolers are notorious for short attention spans, and elementary students' abilities aren't often that much better! This provides an opportunity for our classes to work with a drama/theater teacher or a family and consumer sciences teacher who teaches a child development class. Both of those teachers—and their students—will have beneficial insight into what world language students should do to best hold attention and create a successful storytime program.

Equity in Storytime

Libraries are wonderful distributors of equitable access to resources. They provide access to children's, teen, and adult literature, free of charge. They often provide community meeting spaces and technology access as well, and they're known for free access to educational programming of a variety of types. The American Library Association's website states: *The mission of the American Library Association is to provide leadership for the development, promotion, and improvement of library and information services and the profession of librarianship in order to enhance learning and ensure access to information for all.*

It makes sense to tap into an organization and system that already has a focus on equity and access.

Consider, too, the fact that simply because a resource is technically "free and open to all" doesn't mean that everyone has equal access to it. If you find a library that is open to offering a World Language Storytime, where is it located? Who can most easily access that library? Can families without their own means of transportation easily access the location? If possible, look for a location that is geographically positioned to be inclusive.

Additionally, pay attention to what families will hear about the opportunity and who is less likely to be informed. Is there a way students can market their storytime to families with less access to information? This could also be an opportunity for a cross-curricular project with an art or design class, and there may be methods the library already has in place to increase equitable reach in marketing.

When picking children's books to read, pay attention to the choices, and look for ways to be inclusive. *What countries and/or cultures are included? Whose stories are centered?* Look for a variety, and make sure to consider who is attending the storytime as well as what/who the attendees may never have had exposure to. For example, if the attendees are all from a rural community, try to select one story that includes something they can relate to (e.g., farming, open spaces, homes with yards) and another story that includes something new to them (e.g., skyscrapers, apartment living).

Fortunately, modern authors increasingly include diverse perspectives in children's literature. When I was growing up, characters were largely white, monolingual, of a similar size, and able-bodied. Now, children's sections in libraries include characters of many ethnicities, languages, sizes, and abilities. Including a diverse selection of characters within the books students present is important because it's reflective of the diverse world we live in. Opening eyes to the whole world, rather than a narrow slice, supports children's growth with a global mindset.

Tying Storytime to Global Education Principles

Not only is this an excellent exposure to language and culture for young children, it's a way for the presenters (older students) to **Communicate Ideas** effectively with diverse audiences. What I like best about storytime is that the communication happens in multiple modalities:

> Written: The stories (and often the interlude sections) are part of a slide deck that is projected on a screen.
> Oral: The team presents the stories verbally.
> Physical: When done well, the entire production is quite physical in nature, taking on a theatrical quality.

Storytime is also a way for students to **Take Action**. The action in question is contributing to the literacy development and the global competence of young learners. The young attendees hear and see the TL, which aides in the development of their own TL reading skills. This could also be a useful way to use connections forged with classrooms around the globe. If you're a Portuguese teacher, for instance, your students could partner with an English classroom in São Paulo, each class doing a World Language Storytime in their community. The students in São Paulo could be brought in via video chat to share a story and/or to do one of the interlude activities that your students will then support in real time. Your students could then be similar "guest helpers/presenters" for a World Language Storytime in English in São Paulo. (Of course, when considering the time difference, it may be logistically necessary to use a pre-recorded video in the presentation.) In this way, literacy is supported in two languages on two continents. Learning how to cross-culturally collaborate at a young age supports the creation of adults who have global competence skills that can be useful in the workforce.

With careful consideration of the books that are chosen, this can be a superb way to expose young leaners to different issues, customs, or practices in TL-speaking countries and communities. This supports the **Investigate the World** and **Recognize Perspectives** components at a level that is appropriate for the young learners who attend.

Educator Spotlight: Dr. Frédérique Grim
Position: Professor of French
School: Colorado State University
City, State: Fort Collins, CO

What do your students do for World Language Storytime?

My students have done World Language Storytime in two settings:

1. At the public library
2. At the local French bilingual school

In both cases, students present stories in an interactive way and participate in songs. To prepare for the event, students, in smaller groups, choose a book they like (from a pool of books I share with them) and decide on the format to present it (puppets, costumes and theatrical reading, miming, etc.). On several occasions during the semester, they practice their story in class, receiving feedback from me (the instructor), their peers, and, on occasion, native speakers. I encourage students to think of ways to be interactive within the songs.

Most of the time, I choose the songs (as my repertoire of French children's songs is broader) and share them with the students.

On the day of the presentation, the students perform their stories with a song incorporated between each story. At the library, there is a specific format to follow; while at the bilingual school, it is a little more flexible in how we present (for instance, two stories with only one song).

Why have you chosen this as an activity to include in your class?

Storytime is a wonderful way to practice the language in a unique context. Students have to truly get into the meaning of the story to share it successfully, so it helps with their comprehension. They are also given an opportunity to practice the language in an artistic manner, which meets some of the students' learning style. It also helps them work on their pronunciation as we focus on the comprehensibility of their enunciation. Another very important aspect is that they get the chance to practice their language for an authentic audience, which very often gives them more confidence (although often masked by a little anxiety at first, but once they realize the children are enjoying their stories, they quickly relax and feel more self-confident).

What tips do you have for teachers who would like to participate in something similar?

1. It is important to take time to choose the right books/stories that fit the students, their group dynamic, and their creativity.
2. Help them brainstorm on the presentation of their stories and the techniques and props they want to use.
3. Take time to work on the pronunciation, especially of key words.
4. When you design your course curriculum, plan full sessions to work on this activity.

5. Encourage students to work on props outside of class time, as this could also take a significant amount of time. However, be ready to advise and meet students in your office to help them out.
6. If you have access to native speakers or more advanced speakers, invite them to come listen to the rehearsals as students will have a practice audience and will receive meaningful feedback from non-teachers. (Try to invite guests who might have a less empathic ear due to lack of student exposure.)

What tips do you have for libraries who would like to set up a World Language Storytime at their branch?

1. Libraries should be in touch prior to the semester in order to set a date for the performance and help the instructor plan practices. Communication between the libraries and the instructor is very important.
2. They should be supportive in providing possible stories and props if they have them.
3. Realizing that the event will not happen early in the semester is crucial to support the final performance as it is difficult to get groups of students ready within a few weeks. It is best to plan for the storytime later in the semester, if possible.

How does a project such as World Language Storytime support increased global competence in students?

World Language Storytime presents many facets to exposing our students to global competence. They read and interpret authentic children's literature, which opens up a window to the cultural practices and perspectives of the language they are studying. One great way to do that even further is to offer books that are written by authors from different countries. For instance, with French, countries can include France, Belgium, and Switzerland, but also Canada and many other African countries. Getting our students to read those books gives them an opportunity to be exposed to multicultural perspectives.

In addition, when performing their stories in front of an audience, they meet children and parents who come from a variety of cultural backgrounds. This wealth of relationships develops their global competence within their world.

5

World Language Day at _____

As a child, field trip days were second only to snow days as "Best Day EVER" days. They were special treats—the kind we wished for and the kind we begged our teachers for. Although so much in education has changed since I was a PK-12 student, the love of field trips (or snow days, for that matter!) hasn't changed. The difference, of course, is that now, as a teacher, I know the exhausting work that often goes into planning and executing field trips.

Local museums and attractions, big and small, can attract business by creating unique World Language Days. The Minnesota Zoo in Apple Valley, Minnesota, has been doing that for years and to great success. Each February, the zoo hosts multiple World Language Days (one target language per day), and students come from around the greater Minneapolis–St. Paul metro area to attend.

In advance, the zoo sends registered teachers a list of the animals their students will present, as well as basic information they want included in each presentation. Students then have several weeks to research and prepare presentations for their World Language Day at the zoo. The oldest students there are usually the presenters for animals; the youngest, participants. The zoo provides tables at each exhibit, and the presenters have free reign in their delivery choices. Students typically start with a backdrop presentation board that includes basic information about their animal. From there, though, students can deliver the content and create engagement from the younger attendees in the best way they know how, staying in the target language the whole time. At the end of the day, awards are given for superior presentations in a variety of categories.

The Minnesota Zoo's stated mission is "to connect people, animals, and the natural world to save wildlife." Anyone who has ever taught or has familiarity with Advanced Placement (AP) or International Baccalaureate (IB) curriculum can see firsthand how brilliantly that mission fits in with AP and IB courses.

This type of activity doesn't have to be reserved to zoos. Far from it! Science and art museums, for example, could easily build a parallel program. In each context, the vocabulary is fairly specific, and it often aligns with major concepts that come up in AP and IB, as well as in various textbook scope and sequences. This creates an opening for cross-curricular work with ecology and environmental classes for a zoo or science museum day and with art classes for an art museum day. What could that look like for students in a world language class and a science class to collaborate on an issue of global significance and each, in their own way, disseminate the information?

If you don't have a museum, zoo, or similar business currently hosting World Language Days—and many don't—reach out and ask if they'd be willing to create one. This takes some coordination and planning on the business's part, but they can start small, with just one language, and build after they have a flow. There is incentive for the business to do this, and educational departments of museums often look for ways to engage the community. Furthermore, it can be an effective method to bring in traffic during a traditionally slow time of year...like a zoo...in *Minnesota*...in *February*.

Another route if you don't have a pre-established World Language Day in your area is to do what Dr. William Davis (University of Oklahoma) did when he was teaching high school German in Little Rock, Arkansas. He cold-called area businesses to see if they had any connection to German. Lo and behold, Heifer International had a German volunteer! After a week of teaching key vocabulary, Davis took his German students to Heifer International on a field trip guided entirely in German.

Equity in World Language Day

Although a field trip to a museum isn't a "big ticket item" to many, there are always students for whom it's not financially possible, and it's our responsibility to make sure each student has access. Some schools have funds dedicated to field trip access and equity, but teachers can often easily cover that gap on their own by adding language into the permission slip:

> _____ Enclosed is $X for my student to attend the World Language Day field trip
> _____ Enclosed is $X to support my student and one other to attend the World Language Day field trip

There are so many times parents are looking for ways in which they can support equitable access to field trips, but it's not always clear how to do that. Putting it right on the permission slip is an easy answer. Language can also be added:

> _____ If my support for another student isn't needed, please let me know, and I will revise the amount I am sending.
> _____ If my support for another student isn't needed, please put the amount toward materials needed for the student presentations.

Speaking of materials… Students from all backgrounds and abilities have remarkable creativity and flair, but it requires resources to create presentations that inspire the attendees, judges, and presenters alike. That doesn't always mean that money has to be spent! It takes virtually no time to put out an ask/wish in a Buy Nothing group on Facebook or on Nextdoor. If you're not familiar, both of those platforms are entirely based on neighborhoods. Buy Nothing groups specific to a geographic area exist all over the United States. Members follow strict rules when posting an ask/wish or when "gifting" an item of their own. Everything is a contactless porch pickup. Nextdoor is a social media app that includes a buy/sell component as well as a message board.

Neighbors can post items they're looking for, and writing, "I'm a teacher looking for ____ for a student project" is often be met with offers of "I have some! I'll put it on my steps for you!"

We should also look for diversity in our presentations. If a zoo is hosting a World Language Day, ask for animals that live in countries that span the geographic area of your target language. If an art museum is hosting a World Language Day, speak with the education department about assigning works of art created by men and women, and of people from different ethnicities from different parts of the globe. Ideally, you'd also be assigned artists who speak your target language or are from regions that do.

Tying World Language Day to Global Education Principles

When properly assigned animals (zoo), scientific phenomenon (science museum), or works of art (art museum), students can **Investigate the World**. Particularly when working with teachers and classes of other disciplines, this can lead to more in-depth learning and analysis.

After the investigation piece, students **Communicate Ideas** with a diverse audience of teachers, a wide range of ages of student attendees and staff from the event location. It's easy here to simply disseminate facts, but when the presentation is part of a well-designed unit with requirements that involve more complex analysis and deeper thinking, more *ideas* are shared.

> **Educator Spotlight:** Jo Dougherty
> **Position:** French teacher (current), Japanese teacher (former)
> **School:** formerly at Hastings High School (participated with French students) and Apple Valley High School (participated with Japanese students)
> **City, State:** Hastings, MN; Apple Valley, MN
>
> **What do your students do for World Language Day at the zoo?**
>
> Zoo Day is an opportunity for high school language students to study animal habitats and characteristics, to create a visual and oral

presentation, and to interact with peers (and younger students) in the target language. Groups (of usually four to five students) are assigned a specific animal (by the zoo) to research, and they then create a visual with images showing its location, natural habitat, diet, predator/prey info, interesting characteristics or abilities, etc. They then prepare an oral presentation that may be simply stating facts or, depending on the group, more theatrical like a play, puppet or game show, song and dance number, etc. The presentation ends with observers being asked questions in order to receive a stamp on the "passport" the zoo has given them (that is then most likely collected by the classroom teacher for credit). Again, this may be simply a question or a game for students to play in which they show what they've learned from the presentation. The visiting students may be from elementary to high school level, so preparing a variety of activities is encouraged, as well as varying levels of difficulty, as some of the elementary students who come are from the immersion school and have an impressive level of proficiency (which always shocks the high school students!). Groups of observers rotate through the presentations continuously throughout the day, so presenters are repeatedly performing for new groups.

Why have you chosen this as an activity to include in your class?

Zoo Day is a great way for students to use their language skills not only to create an engaging presentation but also to observe and learn from others in a fun and unique setting. I always loved watching how the presentations evolved throughout the day as students grew more confident and tried new activities and questions with each group. I know for a fact that it was Zoo Day that helped one student realize he wanted to become a teacher…and for others to cement the fact that they DID NOT want to teach! (Maybe it helped them appreciate their teachers more…?)

What tips do you have for teachers who would like to participate in something similar?

If possible, I would allow lower level students to attend Zoo Day as observers, so that they would have ideas for the next year when they became presenters. As some presentations were better than others, it gave them a chance to see what types of activities worked and which didn't. I developed a unit around the experience so that not only was the Zoo Day their summative for the unit, but it helped them be better prepared for the event, as they'd had numerous opportunities to read and speak about animals and their habits. Students did have some class time to research and prepare their presentations, but they were also required to do some preparation of materials outside of class.

What tips do you have for zoos, or similar attractions, who would like to set up a World Language Day?

I would encourage any such attraction with the means to reach out to nearby schools to promote participation in this type of event. It is a wonderful opportunity for collaboration between the community and its schools, and it may open doors for students to consider career opportunities they hadn't previously considered (see teaching comment above). I also had students each year who had never been to a zoo, much less the one in or near their hometown.

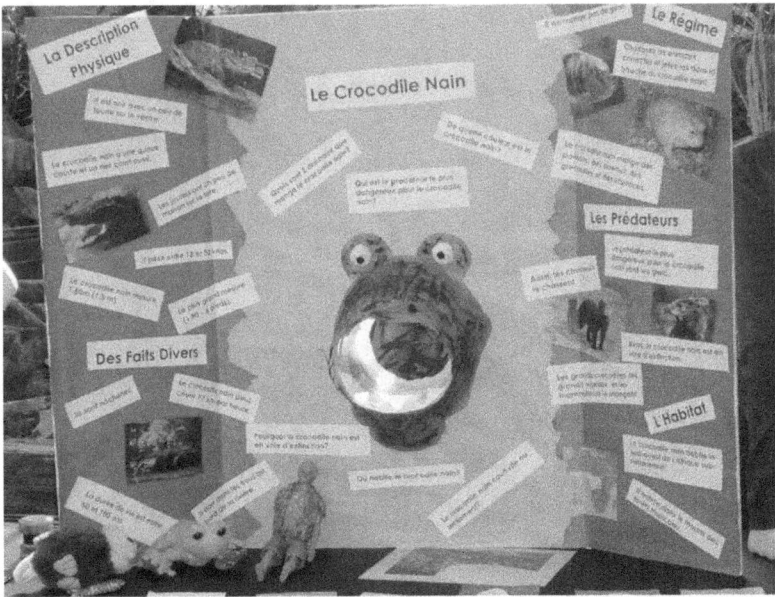

FIGURE 5.1 Student presentation backdrop

How does a project such as World Language Day at the zoo support increased global competence in students?

Because many of the animals assigned to the students are native to other parts of the world, students learn or reinforce knowledge of geography, as well as global issues like climate change and deforestation and the problems they create not only for the animals but for people as well. I always found this unit to be a nice segue into topics like biodiversity and conservation in the environment unit.

6

Empatico

My son is always thrilled for Book Buddy days at his school. His kindergarten class partners with a third grade class, and the third graders read to the kindergarteners. He feels like a "big kid" when he's with *bigger* kids, and I love that the school finds different ways to make literacy development special.

Book Buddies and similar classroom partnerships aren't new, but Empatico allows for a time-tested concept to be taken to a new level. What if those Reading Buddy partnerships were in a different state or even a different country? Enter: Empatico. Empatico's stated mission is "to prepare the next generation for an increasingly connected world in which being able to navigate cross-cultural relationships with empathy is vital for success," and they do that by facilitating partnerships between geographically distant K-8 classrooms.

This educational nonprofit lists its steps as follows: Explore the World, Make Connections, Chat & Schedule, Do Activities, and Have Live Exchanges. (Because of the circular design of their diagram, the Explore the World step can also happen as a result of the exchanges. Therefore, Explore the World can be both the initial step and the final phase. Brilliant!) They use live video chat to allow students and teachers to connect and learn together. Teachers may already have a project in mind that they want to work on collaboratively, but the organization also has its own content library of projects that classrooms can choose from. This is particularly wise, as it allows teachers who may be interested in the concept but who don't yet have their own ideas to participate fully and reap the benefits of cross-cultural connections.

With empathy right there in the mission, this opens up possibilities to bring in other school staff with expertise to support the classroom teachers. For example, a school counselor could work with classroom teachers on units about pillars of character such as responsibility or respect. A reading specialist or school librarian could then select age-appropriate literature that fits content the participating teachers and counselors are covering in their collaboration.

Empatico can be especially great for an immersion or dual-language environment. Students could do science experiments on water quality of local water sources in each community, compare results, and analyze contributing factors, all in the target language. Empatico also opens the door for target language classrooms to connect with English learners around the world and have linguistic exchanges.

Although high school and university classrooms are (as of this publication) not eligible for Empatico projects, the Stevens Initiative is a similar type of organization that includes older students.

Equity in Empatico

The Best Buddies international program and the movement of unified sports teams both work to create partnerships between cognitively and ability-diverse students across the cognitive and ability spectrum. Great partnerships could be made with Empatico in connecting similar populations of students across the world! These connections are made via technology, which allows for support staff, aides, and specialists to be right there with the students as they meet and learn together.

Often, there are opportunity gaps for urban versus rural students. In an urban setting, schools tend to be bigger, which means there are more classes per grade, and there is also a higher number of elementary schools, for example, in a particular geographic area. But in a rural setting, the closest elementary school might be hours away, which can limit opportunities for face-to-face partnerships. With Empatico, all that is needed is a high-speed internet connection! (Admittedly, though we have made global gains in increasing technological access, there is still significant room for improvement.)

One problem world language teachers can run into is providing access to the entire *world* of speakers of the language we teach. We don't want to present a single story (e.g., All Spanish speakers are Mexican), but at the same time, we may not have experience ourselves with all of the different countries in our target language. Often, world language teachers have studied abroad in just one target language country, and depending on finances and opportunity, we may or may not have traveled to others. Empatico allows us to connect and learn from teachers and students in countries we haven't *yet* visited for a fraction of the cost.

Tying Empatico to Global Education Principles

Teaching students to **Investigate the World** is right there in Empatico's steps: Explore the World. Students whose classrooms are in partnerships use video to explore their environs *in real time*. This makes a difference for kids when they know that what they're seeing isn't a movie—it's actually happening in the here and now, just in another part of the world.

Depending on the design and content of the collaboration project, students will **Recognize Perspectives, Communicate Ideas,** and **Take Action** as a natural step in the process. This is where Empatico's support and the cooperating teachers' expertise come into focus. Let's revisit the example of two language immersion classrooms studying and testing local water quality as a part of their science curriculum. After testing, comparing, and analyzing contributing factors, students can work together to create an action plan appropriate to their local contexts.

One of the most valuable pieces of Empatico is that it truly makes it easy for students to learn **with and from the world.**

Instead of *us*, the *teachers*, being the ones to research and tell a particular country's or culture's story (with varying percentages of accuracy), we can rely on teachers and students who are a part of that culture to tell the story. This is a more authentic and rich experience than what we can typically provide alone. Additionally, we can add value and depth to the exchange when the participating classes bring in their own expert from the community to share their story and/or expertise with the students.

Educator Spotlight: Monica Bryant
Position: Elementary School Counselor
School: Linda Givens Elementary School
City, State: Las Vegas, NV

What is your experience with Empatico?

My first experience with Empatico was when they asked NEA Foundation Global Learning Fellows to participate to help spread the word. We were paired with another Global Fellow in West Virginia who taught fifth grade.

Are there ways in which teachers (such as a World Language teacher) partner with other support staff (such as a counselor) on Empatico projects?

Yes! This is exactly what I did! I partnered with a fourth grade teacher that year. Empatico is a perfect way to get school counselors involved because Empatico helps teach about empathy and kindness by partnering classrooms across the nation and globe, and school counselors can help to connect those concepts back to their local communities and school. I also created lessons for us to use during my year that helped teach empathy, which is another great way to involve a school counselor, because we can build lessons to help reinforce the concepts.

What do you think the strengths of Empatico are?

One strength of Empatico is that they pair you up with a class that is not close geographically. I liked this because my students got to experience somewhere they had never been and maybe might not ever go. It was great for them to experience what school was like in a completely different culture. Another strength of Empatico is that they give you lessons and ideas to do with the other class. This is helpful if a teacher is unsure of what to do or how to begin interactions. They are also flexible in that we had ideas we wanted to do that we created ourselves, and Empatico allowed us to do those lessons.

If a teacher is interested in Empatico, what should they do first?

First they should go online to the Empatico website and sign up! Also, if they know other teachers from around the country or globe, encourage them to sign up too! Once they have an account, they can put in to get paired!

How do Empatico projects support increased global competence in students?

Empatico helps students to get to know others who may not look like them and come from a different background, a different geographical area, etc. The more students learn about others with a different background, the more it helps to break down the stereotypes and preconceived notions. It also helps them to gain a more positive view of people in the world, which hopefully builds the kindness and empathy they have for others.

7

ePals

When I was a child, getting mail was one of the more exciting things that could happen in my world. Now that I'm an adult, it turns out that getting *real* mail (not junk mail) *still* is exciting.

The same is true for students, and excitement is amplified when the mail comes from another country…by a person who speaks another language…and has an entirely different culture. Students can—and do—make connections with those their age abroad via social media sites, but a one-to-one relationship is different. It's more exciting and personal; truly, it feels more special. ePals can bring this to life!

Interested teachers can start by creating a free account on the ePals website. There, they can search for a partner teacher/class using a variety of filters: country, student age range, language(s), average class size, subject(s), interest(s), grade(s) taught, or specialization(s). For example, a U.S. Italian teacher could search for a partner classroom in Italy, but they could also search for partners in the Italian-speaking portion of Switzerland or even at an international school on a non-European continent.

Goals are critical for a good match. What are the goals you have for your students and what are the partner teacher's goals? Do they mesh well? A German teacher might want to connect with a German class in another country, but they could just as easily set up a partnership with an English class.

If the teacher connects with another German class, is this a native speaker class? If so, then the class of native speakers could certainly give a lot of support to the German language learners. They would be first-rate peer reviewers for projects, for example. But if the German class partners with another class of German language learners, then everyone is likely at a similar level, which means learning together and sharing successes and failures while doing so. If the partnering German class is at an international school in the Emirates, perhaps, then a rich conversation could be had regarding both classes learning German in non-German-dominate environments. This creates an opportunity for the teachers themselves to share teaching and learning ideas (which can vary wildly from country to country) with each other.

What would it look like for a German class in North America to partner with class of English learners in a German-dominate environment? In this case, the exchanges could be half in German to support the German language learners and half in English to support the English language learners. In this way, each group is an "expert" in one of the languages and a learner in the other. Each exchange could feature one paragraph of helping your pen pal with an English error and/or teaching English vocabulary, as well as one paragraph dedicated to asking cultural or linguistic questions in the language they're learning.

Equity in ePals

Teachers from all corners of the globe create accounts, communicate, and establish partnerships with other teachers who have similar goals. This means that teachers—or even entire classes—can decide where they want to launch those partnerships. They can choose the right partner demographics that fit their and their students' needs. When there is ample opportunity and choice, it's easier to create equitable student experiences.

It's significant that ePals is a free website. As long as the teacher has access to an internet connection somewhere (e.g., school, home, library, etc.), they can make a connection and create an exchange.

We may have a student who has a disability that doesn't allow them to write. Once two teachers establish a connection for their classes, the sky is the limit! The teachers can facilitate snail mail exchanges (writing) or use a digital tool such as Flipgrid to send (video) messages. If video messaging isn't possible, simple audio messages (mp3 or mp4 files) from an entire class can be exchanged in a zip file that the teachers send via email.

Snail mail can be fun to receive, but there's also a cost involved. An alternative is for students to handwrite letters, and then the teacher can scan them all (as one document) and send them via email to the partner teacher. The partner teacher will then print the document and give each of their students the (scanned) handwritten letter from their pen pal.

Tying ePals to Global Education Principles

Pen pals are an easy way to **Investigate the World**, certainly when photos and/or videos are included in the letters and when teachers are specific about what kinds of questions and topics are required. Students could even ask investigatory questions that could be useful in another content area as well.

Especially when teachers guide the letters, students will successfully **Communicate Ideas** about their culture and language with students in other countries who are doing the same. If students ask critical questions and share openly, this communication process also supports learners in **Recognizing Perspectives**.

Educator Spotlight: Jean Slaman-Girard
Position: French teacher
School: Folsom High School
City, State: Folsom, CA

How did you get introduced to ePals?

When I first came up with the idea of doing pen pals with my French students, I put out the question "How do you find pen pals?" in one of my online French teacher groups. I got a bunch of suggestions, and one was to try ePals, so I did.

For what level language class(es) do you use ePals?

I teach French 1 so my classes are mostly grade 9 students. I match them with students in France who are in 3ème—the last year of collège (middle school). I am in California, so French has a hard time competing with Spanish. I thought doing a pen pal exchange would be a good way to interest students in taking French. I find most of the level 1 students to be quite enthusiastic about the project.

How do you and your ePal connection teacher use ePals with your students?

I just used ePals to find a teacher to partner with. I set up a free account and created a profile of what I was looking for. A teacher in France saw my profile and messaged me. We exchanged emails and set up an exchange between our students. We started with snail mail letters between our students, and we also used Padlet to post audio and written messages. The teacher and I communicate using email and Zoom, so we often discuss what we are working on in class. My students write letters mostly in English because they are level 1 and the students in France write in both English and French.

Sometimes my students record in English for her students and hers in French for mine. This gives our students some authentic listening clips.

Recently we were studying classroom vocabulary and the contents of school backpacks. My students took a picture of their contents and wrote a short Padlet post in French to describe. Her students did the same (in French, too, this time), and my students got some good extra vocabulary from their posts. It was also interesting to compare the contents.

Another post which they really enjoy is school lunches. They each post pictures of their lunches and compare the differences between France and the United States. I have also done the same with clothing. They each take a picture of what they are wearing and describe it in the target language. Padlet is fast and easy to use, but the students also enjoy getting the handwritten letters which are more personal. The students also like to connect individually using social media.

What are some tips and tricks you've learned along the way that would help teachers looking to establish an ePals connection?

It is easy to set up a free profile. It is just another way that you can use to find someone to correspond with. You get an email that someone wants to connect with you on ePals. If you feel like the exchange will work, you can then just exchange school emails to discuss how to organize and exchange. We progressed from emails to Zooming together and have also met while I was in France during the summer. I am so glad that I was able to find my exchange teacher because we have worked together for a couple of years. You never know how you will find someone, so the more places that you use to look for someone, the better your chances of finding someone compatible. It might take you a couple of tries before you find someone that you work well with.

How do ePals support increased global competence in students?

The students learn so much from these exchanges. When they receive the snail mail letters, they see that the writing is different and the paper the students use is too. My students make comparisons between their school schedules and the system in France. This is something that is in our textbook, but corresponding with a real person, their age in France really brings it alive. The audio posts are great for authentic listening clips. We have also exchanged videos of our schools. They are more likely to remember this exchange from high school French rather than how to conjugate a verb.

8

International Events in an International Baccalaureate Setting

The first time I heard of the International Baccalaureate (IB) program was in college. A girl in my freshman dorm section talked about coming from an IB school, and I had no idea what she was talking about…and no desire to admit that to her and find out what it was.

Fast forward several years, and I found myself teaching in an IB high school and loving it! Now *I'm* the one who sees the confused faces on others when I say I teach in an IB school. The most common question is, "Is it like Advanced Placement (AP)?" Yes and no. It's like AP in that students can earn college credit based on how well they do on their IB tests. But AP classes have a fixed curriculum set by the College Board, and they are stand-alone courses that students can select. IB, on the other hand, is not a fixed curriculum, and it encompasses the student's entire course of study.

The IB was founded in Switzerland in 1968, and IB schools exist worldwide. An IB diploma is internationally recognized, and the international-mindedness is imbedded into its entire philosophy. From the IB website:

> *We strive to develop students who will build a better world through intercultural understanding and respect, alongside a healthy appetite for learning and excellence.*
>
> *The IB's programmes are different from other curricula because they:*
>
> - *encourage students of all ages to think critically and challenge assumptions*
> - *develop independently of government and national systems, incorporating quality practice from research and our global community of schools*
> - *encourage students of all ages to consider both local and global contexts*
> - *develop multilingual students.*

Although each IB course can vary from school to school, the idea of a global mindset is present throughout the curriculum. Individual teachers can implement global education principles and tools into their courses, but the programs or schools as a whole can also keep the global conversation ever-present.

It is not uncommon for schools, IB or otherwise, to have events such as an International Day/Night. I encourage adults in these spaces to think of ways the traditional event can grow stronger. What if, for example, the event was student-run? How might that change the way the event is organized and perceived? How might that create a different experience for students? The Educator Spotlight in this chapter highlights one such program.

A one-off event could easily expand into a year-long affair. In this way, the international presence is sustained and may more easily become a central part of the school culture. Each month (quarter, semester, etc.) could feature a different area of the world, and the integration could happen throughout the content areas. The recurring event could include guest speakers, themed lunches, and artistic (theater, music, visual arts) presentations. Individual content areas could include data, diverse artistic content, and realia from that area of the world. The possibilities are endless, but the idea is to *keep the conversation going*, to keep international-mindedness *present* and *enjoyable*.

Equity in International Events

There is clear value in providing international events. The time and date they occur, however, can send a clear message of who is welcome. Instead of holding the event during the evening, when many parents and students may have to work, what would it look like if an event (or series of events) were held during the day? That would allow more students to have access. If the organizers wanted to include parents, it would be beneficial to survey parents to determine the best time for them to participate. If the school expanded the event to be year-long, organizers could spread out access to include some events during the day, some after school, and some on weekends.

Another way to make access more equitable is to record the sessions and make them available via video. This could be done in multiple ways. The most labor-intensive would be to live stream each presentation with a Zoom (or other platform) link. It may be equally as effective, not to mention, less work, to have a student simply record each presentation with their phone and put it on a school YouTube channel. In that way, the school could create a library of international-themed talks that could be used at any time by the school, local, state, national, or even international community! (Of course, each teacher who considers this idea will have to consider their specific context and find out whether students would be allowed to be in videos that are uploaded in an online, freely accessible space.)

Tying IB Options to Global Education Principles

The lectures, demonstrations, and/or activities that are present during an international event can easily encompass all four areas of the Asia Society's matrix. Speakers help students **Investigate** the World and **Recognize Perspectives**, particularly when the setup and questions are well constructed and meaningful.

If students are running the event, they are in charge of **Communicating Ideas** with a variety of audiences, in-person and potentially online. There is also an opportunity for follow-up to the event: Students **Communicate** that they learned X, but then they can plan and generate a call to **Take Action** as a direct result of the new knowledge.

Educator Spotlight: Dr. Cori Hixon
Position: IB Director
School: Poudre School District
City, State: Fort Collins, CO

Why do you feel it's important to add global activities/experiences into an IB program?

At its core, IB is focused on humanity and intercultural understanding and respect. The mission statement even emphasizes the importance of students who are "… active, compassionate and lifelong learners who understand that others with their differences, can also be right." In order to fully embrace this mission, students need to physically interact with other people and cultures that may hold different perspectives or ideas. While it is important to include these differing views within the curriculum, global activities and experiences allow students to move beyond their comfort zone and interact with others in a setting that may or may not be familiar.

How do you build an event that is largely student-run?

This requires patience, experience, and students who are passionate about leading and learning. The patience and experience come in recognizing that a successful event takes trial and error over many years. Clearly, knowing what activities and experiences worked in the past helps as you plan for the future. Additionally, word of mouth from one class to the next helps to build the reputation for an event like International Day, for example.

The most important component of building a large event, however, is engaging students who are passionate about teaching others the value of intercultural understanding. These are students who recognize that the world is complex, and different perspectives can be uniting rather than divisive. When the right students work together to organize and implement an event like International Day, the day runs smoothly and participants emerge with a heightened awareness of others.

In your experience, what has worked <u>well</u> when planning global-themed events?

The most successful International Days were those in which our own students were enlisted as presenters. Drawing on our student population to highlight various cultures and traditions validated their individual experiences, thus strengthening our community.

In your experience, what has <u>not</u> worked well when planning global-themed events?

For the first few years I did this, we used speakers from the university who had expert knowledge on cultures and traditions. While nearly all of the speakers represented a multicultural perspective, they did not have a relationship with the school or students. Unfortunately, the high school students saw this as a day of lectures rather than a day to interact and appreciate cultures and traditions different from their own. Ultimately, relationships and relevance are the keys to a successful event.

Do you have tips to share on how to make global activities authentic and valuable?

I think it's important to engage students in the organization and implementation of the event. Draw on the resources and expertise of those within the school, and allow the students to showcase their cultures and traditions. This validates the experiences of students from the non-majority culture and enhances the shared experiences of all students.

9

International Student Panel

We tend to think that the "world" is out "there." While there is truth to the fact that the sheer mass of the area we have to explore on our planet is considerable, it is also true that we frequently miss what's right under our noses. Increasingly, the "world" is part of our day-to-day interactions. Schools, for example, regularly neglect the wealth of knowledge that resides in our international students and newcomer Americans.

In the first high school I ever worked, we held a yearly event called the International Student Panel. This was a cooperation between all the world language classes and the teacher of English language learners, some of whom were international students and some of whom were newcomers.

Every world language class was assigned a different category: food, customs, education, driving, holidays, or family, to name a few. Then the class would generate a list of questions that they'd like to know the answers to and that pertained to the countries represented by the international students at the school that year. One student would be elected as the class representative.

On Panel Day, all the language classes would file into the auditorium, and the class representatives would take a seat on the stage. In between the representatives would be special spots for the international students participating in the panel. In front of them would be a card with their name and country of origin.

The representatives would take turns asking a question that their class generated, and the international students would pass a microphone down the line, responding to each question, but also having the option to "pass." Meanwhile, students in the audience had a handout for notes.

Was this activity perfect? No. The question categories were mainly at the surface level of culture, and both the question categories and the time frame didn't permit us to probe very far. I also regret that there was no follow-up, no continuing relationship among the classes and the students. A continuing relationship could've given us more time to ask deeper questions and hear more of their story, if they wanted to share.

But did this activity establish connections? Absolutely. As a direct result, students in the world language classes knew some of the international students by name and could—and did—greet them in the hallways or make connections in other classes or during lunch. The international students truly had a chance to shine, and for the most part, the world language students were interested listeners, and the class reps asked their class's questions in clear ways and kept the dialog moving. Everyone had some great laughs too, especially when students shared their true feelings about certain American foods—there wasn't much middle ground, as far as opinions went!

Any similarly structured activity can benefit all learners in the room. Academically, the world language students learned about other places in the world directly from students their own age, and the international students and newcomers got practice their language skills. Socially, however, the relationships were more important. The panel allowed students who have never left the United States to have genuine contact and make connections with students whose countries of origin they likely only saw on the news. This is one of the most vital seeds needed for the development of empathy.

Equity in Student Panels

Arguably the most crucial aspect of the student panel is the fact that it gives a voice to international and newcomer students.

How, precisely, that voice is given and expressed should be led by the international/newcomer students, not by students of the dominate culture. They can work with their teacher to determine what's important to them, what stories they'd like to share, and what topics they're comfortable discussing with their language skills.

Tying Student Panels to Global Education Principles

With the right questions, the panel is perfect for **Recognizing Perspectives**. The more advanced the panel participants are in the dominant language of the school (which is presumably the language of the presentation), the more critical thinking can occur around how the context of the student or country of origin shaped the perspective. If the panel is set up less like a Q&A session and more like a dialog, topics could be discussed much more deeply.

> **Educator Spotlight:** Anne Muske
> **Position:** French Teacher
> **School:** Lakeville South High School
> **City, State:** Lakeville, MN
>
> **How did the International Student Panel come to be?**
>
> In 2002, when I began working at Lakeville High School (before Lakeville South High School opened), I think the International Student Panel already existed. I took over when we decided to host the event in conjunction with National French Week.
>
> **How do you think participation in the panel benefits students on the panel? What changes do you see post-activity?**
>
> The original format was international students sitting on the panel all day long while different students from the various classes attending the event joined them each hour. The world language class students asked questions on a variety of topics, and the international students took turns answering. Each world language class was assigned a topic

to avoid repetition of questions. The goal wasn't so much to benefit students on the panel. It was to expose the audience members to students from beyond our city. It undoubtedly did benefit the students on the panel, however, as they gained "fame." As a result of the event, many more students knew who they were. I think the world language students were less shy about approaching the international students after seeing them on the panel.

Are there tips and tricks you've learned along the way that would help teachers to establish a similar activity on their campuses?

We eventually switched from panel to presentation. We no longer invite the world language students onto the stage to ask the questions. Instead, we provide the questions to the international students and ask them to prepare a slide deck presentation containing at least ten interesting things. We have a student serve as emcee for the event, and each international student is introduced via a video, either a tourism video or a singer from their country, of their choosing.

How does this activity support increased global competence in students?

It piques the world language students' curiosity about other people and places, and it helps the world language students realize they don't need to fear people who are different from themselves.

10

Video Options

In the 21st century, the extent to which new careers are created is astonishing. It's now not uncommon for students to reply "Content creator!" or "Influencer!" when asked what they want to be when they grow up or what they want to do after graduation. This underscores the fact that students like creating videos, and more often than not, they're good at it! So why not put that to educational use?

I'll use an example from my own classroom. In 2017, I met Dr. Joe Underwood, who is featured in this chapter's Educator Spotlight. I teach French, and he taught video production. I was inspired by the remarkable stories of his students and their work in highlighting the Sustainable Development Goals (SDGs), and I thought we could build a partnership.

My International Baccalaureate (IB) French 4/5 class was studying Global Issues, a prescribed IB topic at the time. Students worked in groups, and they were tasked with finding an issue of interest to them that relates to an SDG and that exists in a francophone country. They had to research the issue and propose a way for the class to play a part in supporting the community or country in which the problem existed.

After the research and planning phase, students presented their proposals to the class in French. Each student voted on which proposal they thought had the most potential, the one they would like to work on as a class. The only stipulation was that they couldn't vote for their own group.

The presentations blew me away. I provided little-to-no guidance, yet the students had diverse ideas and did an excellent job trying to convince their classmates of the merit of their group's idea.

The class ended up choosing the clean water shortage in Haiti as their issue, and they wanted to raise funds for Pure Water for the World, an organization that creates safe water solutions in rural and underserved communities in Haiti and Honduras. This linked to SDG 6: Clean Water & Sanitation.

We chose to create a video with Dr. Underwood's video production class. My class wrote the script—in both English and French—and gathered images, supporting data, sound files, and documentation for the video production team. Dr. Underwood's class then produced a bilingual video and uploaded it to YouTube. One of the jobs assigned to my students was "social media specialists," and they were tasked with creating a variety of social media posts for students in both classes to use to share with their networks. On our end, each day in class, we would use a quick two minutes in class for students to post their "social media blast" on whatever platform they chose. It could also be simpler, like emailing info to friends and family members.

This type of project was easy to carry out long distance with my school in Colorado and Dr. Underwood's school in Florida. When the video was done, each class shared it as far and wide as they could, and we raised several hundred dollars for Pure Water for the World. Additionally, Dr. Underwood's class made a version in Spanish, using our script, and shared that with their Spanish-speaking population. I believe the students felt like they made a difference, and I even received an email from a parent thanking me for the project.

Equity in Video Options

What I especially love about video production is the fact that there are many roles for students to play in the process, such as:

writer, actor (voice or otherwise), video recorder, video editor, uploader, and social media "influencer" to promote the videos. The array of jobs highlights a variety of skills that can be found in our students. Some of these jobs can be done individually, and some are better suited to group work. Because of this range, we have a greater opportunity for students to shine in their strengths or, conversely, for students to push themselves in learning a new skill.

Creating content doesn't require new funds. Typically, the cameras students already have on their phones, combined with a good internet connection either at home or in school, are all that is needed to bring projects to life.

Additionally, teaching students the skills used in video production are skills that students could use in a future job. (Note: The world language teacher doesn't have to be the one to teach these skills. This is a perfect opportunity for the media specialist to do a lesson in our class.) Not every student has the means to attend college—and not every student *wants* to—but equipping our students with 21st-century skills during PK-12 is never *not* worth our time and frequently supports student growth and future success.

Tying Video Options to Global Education Principles

Technology provides students a means and a platform to **Communicate Ideas** with diverse audiences around the globe. The internet makes it possible for those same ideas to catch fire and spread! Students can communicate in their first or second (or more!) language, and depending on the medium for sharing, the communication can turn into a dialog with global participation.

Student videos can also contain a critical component to improve the world: a call to action. Students of all ages can see problems quicker than teachers give them credit, and they can develop solutions that teachers often don't see coming. Students are naturals at **Taking Action**.

Educator Spotlight: Dr. Joe Underwood, EdD, ATC
Position: Television Production Teacher, Athletic Trainer (retired)
School: Miami High School
City, State: Miami, FL

Why did you choose to integrate the SDGs into your teaching?

In 2017, I was honored to be selected as a NEA Foundation Global Fellow. This immense recognition included a year-long professional development with 45 other elite educators from across the nation representing 45 states. The NEA Foundation Global Fellows concentrated their efforts on global issues and especially on the SDGs of the United Nations and the history and culture of South Africa. The Global Fellows collaborated in writing a published curriculum in conjunction with Harvard professor, Dr. Fernando Reimers, and culminated their year of study with an educational adventure to South Africa where they were immersed in South African culture and history.

Upon my return to my television production classroom at Miami Senior High School following our experience in South Africa, I introduced the SDGs to my advanced television students, and they were quite interested in pursuing research in many areas presented by the SDGs. For the students, this was a welcome change of our approach to becoming globally competent since they had been researching, writing, and producing video reports for a project entitled "Square in the World," which focused on various public squares around the globe and the history behind them. Turning our attention to the SDGs allowed them to tackle in-depth issues that appealed to them.

How did you integrate the SDGs into your classes?

After introducing the SDGs to my advanced television students (the Miami High MovieMakers), I asked them to look more closely at each SDG and to decide in which area(s) they were interested. This was going to be an ongoing project, and I wanted my students to address more than one area of concern. They were to work in partnership with other students because in television production there are several areas that need to be addressed to have a successful outcome: research, scriptwriting, voice-over, and editing. Graphics was another important component. All of our video reports were designed to be short enough to (1) fit into our daily, ten-minute live television broadcast as an educational tool, and (2) keep students from becoming disinterested due to lengthy writing and editing sessions.

Tell me about the partnerships you had with other teachers/classes.

Collaboration with other educators around the country, and the world for that matter, has always been important in my teaching career at Miami High. The NEA Foundation global competency project that began with our year-long professional development before heading to South Africa allowed all of our NEA Foundation Global Fellows to get to know each other and our approach to teaching. Since we all came from different areas of study on many levels from K-12, it was richly rewarding for my students to collaborate with not one, but three of my fellow Global Fellows as the Miami High MovieMakers brought to life video reports on the efforts of middle school students cleaning up a river in Ohio, on clean water in Haiti with a group of advanced French class students in Colorado, and a teacher–student collaboration between one of my television students in Miami and a teacher of indigenous language in Alaska. Communicating, collaborating, and producing videos not only help students and teachers learn from each other, but it also brought our SDG community closer regardless of where in the world we might be.

Previously, in 2006, I was honored to be selected by the Toyota International Teacher Program to visit the Galapagos Islands with eight other outstanding educators from around the United States, one of which was another Miami-Dade County Public Schools (MDCPS) teacher like myself. One of our goals in visiting the remote archipelago was to collaborate with Galapagueño teachers by presenting to them on various issues, and they would present to us. Our U.S. contingent was divided into two groups of four, and our group decided that our presentation would be on the specter of invasive species in the United States and finding out about invasive species in the Galapagos Islands. It was an eye-opening experience to learn that goats and blackberry plants were plainly the most concerning issue in the Galapagos. This was truly a learning experience for all of us, especially since we were undertaking our group effort on a new and lightly used technology called "the internet." Somehow, we managed to complete our project with this unfamiliar telecommunication tool.

(Author's note: The stories above are just a sample. Dr. Underwood had many other collaborations with teachers across the United States!)

How did your students react to the work with the SDGs?

My high school television students were quite enthusiastic about our new focus on the SDGs presented by the United Nations. My promotion of U.S. and global learning had been part and parcel of my television curriculum since being named a Disney All-American Teacher Honoree (then called the DisneyHand Awards) in 2004. It was a life-changing experience for me, and it helped me to change the lives of my students in a positive manner for the rest of my teaching career. Our daily, live television newscast has always strived to bring educational content to our viewers. After having worked on and completed dozens of "Square in the World" video reports, the students were anxious to try something new. Introducing SDGs to them opened their eyes and imaginations, giving them more flexibility to explore more important topics than simply describing the history and significance of public meeting places around the world, although that research did lead to students wanting to visit many different cities when they saw what other students were producing.

Now students could turn their attention to truly important topics such as poverty, health, education, gender equality, climate, and more as they undertook the challenges of researching, writing, and collecting video and photos to edit into a short but comprehensive message that the students selected themselves. Some of these reports were also completed in Spanish since a large majority of our student population is Spanish-speaking.

Student interest in the SDG project became more intense the more they produced their own videos. My students seemed to be searching for more ways to address global issues. Their enthusiasm was evident in the fact that they embraced these challenges and produced over 50 SDG video reports all with the tag line, "I'm (name) and I am becoming globally competent." I purposely kept them from stating that they were globally competent, because they were not, but through their collaborative efforts of research, planning, and post-production, my students were working in a confident manner toward becoming globally competent, and they were displaying a plethora of worldwide issues and concerns to their 3,000-student audience on a daily basis on *Stingtown News*. Their videos were also posted on YouTube.

What effect do you think global education-focused lessons had on students? How do you know?

Teachers often just know when their proposed projects are a success (or failure) with their students. When it came to student reaction to our Global Competency project based on the SDGs, I was confident that my Miami High MovieMakers had not only made an impact, but they were enjoying the process. They were meeting more deadlines;

they were working in groups at their own pace. Researchers were researching, writers were writing, and editors were editing. Teachers were making positive comments on the videos they had seen on *Stingtown News* that sparked their interest.

Reluctant students were showing interest and working diligently toward self-improvement. Two examples stand out. Both were male students and had trouble in my television class because of their ability, or lack thereof, to properly enunciate when recording a voice-over. All of the Global Competence videos include voice-overs. This ability to properly communicate with words and phrases is critically important in television production. One of the students, a Nicaraguan and a leader in the class, was well known for slurring his words. The other student, from Honduras, spoke extremely quickly and in a sort of gibberish that made him sound like Latka Gravas, the fictional character on the television show "Taxi." These students not only worked hard to overcome their communication skills in producing their Global Competency videos but astounded both myself and my students with the final outcome.

More importantly, my students embraced our project so much that many of them recorded original footage in several countries. The Nicaraguan student visited Nicaragua to see family and brought back some amazing footage of poverty and need. Still, with his slurred speech we had a problem. His girlfriend was part of his production team and was usually the one who recorded voice-overs for their projects. On this particular segment, however, he wanted to perform the voice-over. I encouraged him to do so with the stipulation that his girlfriend would be his producer and voice coach. He did not take that advice well at the beginning. He did not like the idea of a female having production control over him, but he finally relented. To say that I was blown away by his final video would be an understatement. His voice was clear and understandable. His emotion was heartfelt when he described his homeland.

The Honduran student continued to struggle with slowing down and articulating his vocal delivery, but he did not give up. He decided his SDG video was going to be based on SDG 8: Decent Work and Economic Growth. How this young man found footage of a shipyard graveyard in Bangladesh is beyond my comprehension (of course, how many of my students came up with their footage was also a mystery that I did not want to solve—teenagers are very adept with technology research). His story was about the workers in this shipping graveyard who deconstruct huge oceangoing vessels for scrap. They work in horrendous conditions carrying thousand-pound pieces of steel through muddy waters—barefoot—to the smelter. These workers are paid little and are often subject to extremely dangerous conditions. There was even a shot of a worker falling from a ship into the muddy waters below. More importantly, however, was the voice-over that accompanied his project. He had worked long and hard at slowing down, and his pronunciation was amazing, not to just me but to our entire class. It earned him a standing ovation from the other students, and at the end of the year he received a WMHS Most Improved Student award. This is how I know my students not only enjoyed the Global Competency projects but immersed themselves in finding out more and more about the SDGs.

Another way that was seen as a positive reaction to the SDG project was the amount of original footage that my students recorded on some of their international trips. These students are not wealthy and flying around the world for fun; they are often going back to their homeland to visit family and friends. We also had footage from several students who returned to Cuba, although this footage had to be clandestinely recorded in many cases. There was some other original video recorded in Haiti and Puerto Rico. There is one exception to the visit to her homeland as one young lady has an older sister who is a flight attendant who travels internationally. The flight attendant rewarded her little sister with a trip to Greece. While in Greece, my student took time to record video that she planned on using in her television production class at Miami High.

11

Podcasts

"It's the modern version of the old radio programs that families would crowd around in the 1920s and 1930s." That's what I tell my dad, the most technology-averse person I know, when he asks me what a podcast is.

Podcasts offer a never-ending library of content in the target language because new episodes are added daily. Many are accessible through the major podcast platforms (e.g., Apple Podcasts, Audible), so students can download them onto their phones, but it's wise to search online as well, as some international podcasts may not be on the major North American platforms yet.

Some podcasts are made expressly for language learners, so those are appropriate choices for the novice-level learners, and they may often produce content that fits directly with major units of study. As students progress, however, it becomes increasingly easy to use podcasts geared toward native speakers.

There are several ways teachers can use podcasts in classrooms. Students can listen on their own to a podcast of choice or an assigned episode, or the entire class could listen together to the same episode. Podcasts can be useful for subplans as well. If you're in an International Baccalaureate school, podcast episodes are typically long enough to fit the length requirements for listening assessments.

A fun option is setting up clubs—like book clubs, but for podcasts. For that strategy, the teacher finds different podcasts to propose to the class. They may have different topics, be at different language levels, or be from different countries in the target language world. Students can self-select into a group, and every Monday, for example, class starts with "Podcast Club." The students meet with their "club," listen to and discuss the podcast together, and do the activity the teacher has created for the clubs.

Equity in Podcasts

When we search for podcasts, it's critical to think about accessibility as well as content. An appropriate place to start is looking for podcasts that have an option to slow down the speech. This supports language learners across the spectrum: Newer or more hesitant learners can slow it down (often considerably), while heritage speakers might even want to speed it up, just to maximize their time and get through the content faster.

Podcasts that are specifically produced for language learners may also have transcripts available. Transcripts can support students with Individualized Education Programs (IEPs) or 504 plans, but there are also activities we can create that blend receptive (listening, reading) language skills.

We can also consider the perspectives chosen. To the extent possible, we should search for perspectives from a variety of countries or regions in which the target language is spoken. This helps diversify perspectives instead of focusing on a single (geographic) story, but it also allows students time with different accents and vocabulary. If we have heritage speakers in our classes, it can feel uniquely special for those learners to connect with podcasts from the country of their family's origin.

Tying Podcasts to Global Education Principles

Depending on the podcast topic, the content could be rich for **Investigating the World** and **Recognizing Perspectives**. Because there are a variety of podcasts available, including, seemingly, new ones every week, teachers can do simple searches for themes and information relevant to what they're studying in class and what kind of discussion they hope to foster among students.

But why stop with receptive language? Students can **Communicate Ideas** by *producing their own podcast!* There isn't much equipment needed, and there are free videos to walk new podcasters through the process. No class time? Try it as a project for a language club!

Educator Spotlight: Mary Beth Johnson
Position: Spanish Teacher/Teaching and Learning Facilitator—World Language
School: Poudre School District
City, State: Fort Collins, CO

What podcasts produced by native speakers have you used and in what classes?

Radioambulante—IB Spanish 5, Spanish Literacy 5
Duolingo Podcast—IB Spanish 4 and 5

How do you use podcasts in your classes?

I have used these podcasts as anchor texts for thematic units and for options for my students' weekly listening logs that they do outside of class.

What are some tips and tricks to finding, vetting, and/or using podcasts?

The main way I find podcasts is by listening to lots of podcasts myself. Every time I hear one I think would fit with a unit I have taught or would like to teach, I try to save the link in the resource folder I keep in my Google Drive. I also search the databases of podcasts I trust for keywords related to the themes I am teaching.

How can podcasts be used with students of different language abilities? Or are there some podcasts that are better at that than others?

The Duolingo podcast has some scaffolding built in, with parts of the episodes in Spanish and parts in English. It is designed for intermediate learners.

For Radioambulante, I like to give students a menu of options and let them pick the level of scaffolding that works for them. My classes are a mix of native/heritage speakers and second language students, so there is a wide range of abilities. The students with the highest proficiency levels may be listening to the podcast on their own and writing a summary, looking for examples of the theme we are studying, or creating an outline. Other students may choose to listen and read the transcript along with it. Some may choose to slow down the rate of speech while they listen. Sometimes I go over the basics of the podcast with them first in language I know they will understand so that they have the big idea before they start listening. Sometimes we use guided notes as we listen to help students identify main ideas and key details.

How does this resource support increased global competence in students?

What I love about podcasts is that they often give students a firsthand account of a global story or global issue. Being able to listen to someone's personal story creates empathy and connection, two things that I believe to be foundational in developing global competence.

12

Window Swap

The eyes are the "window to the soul." Language is often referred to as a "window to culture." What, then, is an actual *window* a window to?

Window Swap allows students to literally see out a window somewhere in the world, but it's not simply a photograph—we actually can see what's *happening* out that window!

Similar to podcasts, teachers can certainly implement Window Swap as a whole class activity with everyone looking out the same window, or it can be an individual or small group activity with each student or group looking out a different window. The latter option will depend on the number of devices in the classroom. Always take into account that each window only lasts ten minutes before a new one automatically comes on. To stop the changing/looping, click on "loop off."

Here are a few ways we can use Window Swap in class:

Full class: Start each class (or each Wednesday's class, for example) with Window Swap. Students will see that day's window projected on the classroom screen, but the teacher will have covered the window owner's name and location. From there, students start by describing everything they see. This is an excellent opportunity to use sentence starter lists that are tailored to the appropriate proficiency level. After students describe the scene, they start to make predictions about where the scene might be and give justifications for that prediction. (More sentence starters!) The teacher can then reveal the name of the window's owner, and the class can talk about the scene in the context of that owner. For example, if the scene shows a backyard with a fruit tree, perhaps *José is going to eat fresh fruit today* is logical. Lastly, where are we? The teacher reveals the location, and the class discusses:

How are we similar?

How are we different?

How are we interconnected? (This may require some quick research.)

Small group (one device per group): Give each group X minutes to write what they see on a piece of butcher paper using the target language. While students write, the teacher will write a letter at the top of each piece of paper and put a Post-it Note with a number on each computer screen. When time is called, students hang up their posters around the room and travel around, looking at the windows and matching the image number to the description letter.

Partners (one device needed): Partners sit facing each other. Partner A has a window up and gets X minutes to describe the window scene to Partner B, who draws the scene, based on the info given. At the end of the X minutes, the partners put the drawing and the window image next to each other to compare before switching roles.

An entertaining complement to Window Swap is Radio Garden. On this site, users can turn the globe and click on any of the thousands of illuminated dots which play music from that city/country! This is a simple way to make the activity more immersive. (The only potential obstacle is that many countries' radio stations play American music…uncensored. Depending on your school, this could pose a problem.)

Equity in Window Swap

Window Swap is an excellent educational tool not only because of what it provides but because of the cost. There is a free version and a paid version, the latter of which is only $5/month.

Parents often like to know how they can support their student's classroom, so a "1-month of Window Swap" gift would be a useful wish list item at the beginning of the school year.

Tying Window Swap to Global Education Principles

Window Swap allows students to **Investigate the World**. This website can be a perfect introduction to an area of the world your class is studying, a jumping-off point to start deeper conversations and study.

Educator Spotlight: Sunny Cordray
Position: Spanish Teacher
School: Forsyth Country Day School
City, State: Lewisville, NC

How do you use Window Swap in your classes?

I use Window Swap for conversation starters, for a story starter, and to compare and contrast aspects of life in different countries. It can be a five- to ten-minute warm-up or something much deeper. My students all say that it is fun.

When doing activities with Window Swap, what have students noticed or shared that stood out to you?

Students love that every window is a surprise! They never know what the view might be like. Everyone is engaged and they are intrigued to see how life can be so different and yet the same in other countries. They make observations about the weather, city versus country living, standard of living, clothing, and geography, and they are able to reflect on their own place in the world. Sometimes we play "I Spy" games or guess the continent games, other times they do a free write about what they see. Students always get excited to explore the world and to imagine the possibilities.

How could Window Swap be beneficial at different levels of language learning?

Window Swap is the perfect starting place for all levels of language. Students can use single words to describe what they see or they can create a story imagining what takes place outside the window in a city. Window Swap makes the culture and lifestyle of different areas come alive!

Are there tips and tricks to using Window Swap that would be helpful for a teacher who has never used it to know?

It is free and easy to use. It can be used on students' individual computers, and they can pick their own city in the world, or you can lead a class activity. Also, you can decide if you want the sound on or off. It is very user-friendly!

How does using Window Swap support increased global competence in students?

Window Swap provides students with an easy way to investigate the world and to share perspectives about different cultures. I think Window Swap gives students a glimpse into areas of our world they might never see otherwise and it makes them feel more connected to others. Being an engaged citizen of the world is key, and Window Swap is a great starting place!

13

City Walks

Roam, if you want to…roam around the world! The B-52s' "Roam" hit the airwaves in 1989, well before City Walks (and the internet) existed, but they were certainly onto something. Roaming around a new city, with no time frame and no agenda, is one of the top ways to experience culture and expand global competence.

City Walks is a website that creates explorations through its list of global cities. Users can toggle for a daytime or nighttime walk and choose a walk with or without sound. There's even an option to experience a walk during COVID-19! City Walks puts the user in the walker's place, their camera becoming our eyes.

The same full-class, individual, or small group activities that classes can do with Window Swap (Chapter 12) can also be done with City Walks, though there's more to see during a City Walk, so the activities could easily take more time. Chapter 10 highlighted video options, and a logical project is to have a class create their own City (or Neighborhood) Walks, narrate them in the target language, and then post them on a class YouTube channel. (Not sure how to do that? There are easy online videos that walk a user through it, but my first stop is always with my school media specialist.)

When using City Walks, consider ways to spice it up! There are benefits to allowing the sounds to play during the City Walks themselves, but it can also be fun to listen to local music while roaming the streets. Radiooooo is a free website in which you can click on a country in the map and then click on a specific decade to hear music popular in that country in that decade!

Another option to spice things up is to, well…add spice! One of the best aspects of walking through the streets while traveling is the smell of the local fare wafting out of restaurants and bakeries. The opportunity for collaboration with foods classes is ripe! Imagine students in a Chinese class doing a City Walk in Shanghai when all of a sudden, the Catering 2 class enters with platters of fresh dumplings! The smell fills the air, students' senses are ignited, and the "trip" becomes better yet!

An alternative to City Walks is using Pegman (the small, yellow human figure) in Google Maps. A Portuguese teacher, for instance, could give students the addresses of different landmarks in Portugal and Brazil. Students then can enter the address into Google Maps and drag and drop Pegman onto the street in front of the landmark. From there, they can navigate up and down the streets on their own. The *pro* is that students can do the exploring, and they can explore anywhere Google has sent their car. The *con* is that it's slower than City Walks and is a more static experience.

Equity in City Walks

City Walks, like the virtual reality systems in Chapter 21, are cheaper means by which students can "visit" the world. It's hard to substitute a screen of any type for actually traveling, so some may scoff at the idea of this type of "fake" travel. When we downplay a virtual trip in our heads, it's crucial to ask ourselves, "Why do I feel this way? Why do I think it's not good enough?" The answer, usually, is because we *have* traveled, and we know every bit of how amazing a change of geography can be! What a wonderful privilege we have had to travel. We must, however, consider (at least) two key points with our students:

1. Some students have never left their *city*—or, for some, their *neighborhood*—so a virtual trip can be more exciting than a well-seasoned traveler could ever know.

2. Some students *can't* travel. It may be that they have severe physical needs that would be difficult or cost-prohibitive to meet in another country, or perhaps their anxiety is so high that their mental health would deteriorate with travel. For these students, we must consider equitable alternatives.

City Walks is, remarkably, a free website. This makes it easier for students to explore both in and outside of class, as long as they have internet access.

Just because we teach a specific language doesn't mean students wouldn't benefit from doing a City Walk in a location that *doesn't* speak that language. World exploration benefits learners, no matter the language. Furthermore, exploring a variety of countries allows students with a myriad of backgrounds to see world citizens who look like them and their families.

Tying City Walks to Global Education Principles

Just like Window Swap, City Walks allows students to **Investigate the World**. Because of the sheer volume of visual stimuli, it's an excellent tool for inter- and intra-cultural comparing and contrasting.

> **Educator Spotlight:** Peter Dola
> **Position:** Lecturer in French; Department of Languages, Literatures, and Cultures
> **School:** The University of North Carolina at Greensboro
> **City, State:** Greensboro, NC
>
> **How do you use City Walks in your classes?**
>
> I use City Walks to teach grammar, and the vocabulary of geography, names of countries, and cities. I take turns with my students and model what they can do in small groups, or ideally, with partners. I asked my students, "How would you feel walking alone on the streets of an unknown city in a foreign country? Use three adjectives."

We play Battleship-like games, with each student going on City Walks, and without seeing their partner's screen, students take turns giving each other directions and guiding each other.

Other times, I may instruct my students any of the following:

- View a foreign city in City Walks, and share three things about what you notice in the video with a partner or in a small group.
- Describe the physical characteristics of this city walk. How are they similar to or different from the city in which you live?
- Write a summary of your most interesting findings in your city walk.
- Write one opinion about this location.
- Compare and contrast, identify similarities and differences, between the streets in your hometown with those of another city in City Walks.
- Write a journal entry using sensory details to describe a walk in a foreign city in City Walks.

The imperative is often introduced in the context of asking and giving directions. After teaching my students how to form the imperative in the target language, I instructed them to go to City Walks and asked them, "¿Cómo se llega a... desde...?, "Comment arrivez-vous à... de...?", "How do you get to...from...?"

When doing activities with City Walks, what have students noticed or shared that stood out to you?

Students noticed that life seems to go by pretty slowly in several foreign cities in City Walks. Especially in the small towns, people are in a more relaxed mood, people take their sweet time enjoying conversation at sidewalk cafés, and not many people seem stressed or in a rush like in large American cities with the hustle and bustle.

Students shared that in their American hometowns, there are fewer pedestrians, and the streets are often deserted at night. Whereas in many foreign cities in City Walks, you see pedestrians strolling the streets at all times of the day, even late at night.

Students noticed that in several foreign cities, there are no lanes on the roads, no street lights, and no crosswalks, and cars do not yield to pedestrians.

How could City Walks be beneficial at different levels of language learning?

At the beginner's level, I instruct my students:

- ♦ Using the target language, choose three adjectives to best describe this City Walk.
- ♦ Write one synonym and one antonym for each of the three adjectives you choose.
- ♦ List three nouns you see in this location.
- ♦ List three verbs you see in this location.
- ♦ Write a simile or metaphor describing this location.
- ♦ Identify, list, and share three interesting things you observe in the city walk. It might be something similar to or different from your American hometown or just an interesting feature such as a type of shop or a sign.

At the intermediate level, I instruct my students to imagine they are on vacation in this location:

- ♦ Write a personal letter to a family member or friend using sensory details to describe your city walk.

Are there tips and tricks to using City Walks that would be helpful for a teacher who has never used it to know?

This free website allows your students to explore the globe safely on foot. You can pick a city, turn on the sound if you want street noise, and select a daytime tour or a nighttime tour.

This website was created by Aristomenis Georgiopoulos and Artemis Stiga, a real-life couple that loves traveling. They encourage their website visitors to "Walk around cities of the world, day or night, on a pre- or post-Covid period, and listen to the sounds of the city."

How does using City Walks support increased global competence in students?

There is much of the world to see and to talk about on City Walks for world language teachers and their students. Because of its high-quality videos and easy handling, City Walks is a perfect pedagogical tool for the language classroom. It allows teachers to teach discrete grammar points and culture in a natural context that is as real as it can get in the classroom.

After going on virtual City Walks in Mecca (Saudi Arabia), Marrakech (Morocco), Dubai (United Arab Emirates), and Tehran (Iran), one of my students noticed the different ways men and women dressed (the hijab, the burka), and that during Ramadan almost all restaurants and many shops were closed from sunrise to sunset. The student learns that for people of those countries, fasting is something that they do every year, along with their families and religious community. He also learns that fasting is significant because it is a way of demonstrating control over your body. He recognizes that the themes of community, sacrifice, and material transcendence are common to many different religions. Through City Walks, the student better understands the perspectives of other religions and his respect for religious diversity increases.

14

News in Slow _____

One of the chief by-products of travel and of creating connections around the world is that we become more interested in what happens in the rest of the world. We begin to understand more fully how intimately connected we are to each and every human, and because of that, we care about the well-being of those on the opposite side of the world—people we don't know and likely will never know.

We can guide students in their education about world affairs by incorporating News in Slow _____ (NIS) into our classes. In their own words, NIS is "A streaming service for language immersion, created and produced by an international team of journalists, writers, linguists, audio engineers, and native language hosts." As of this publication, the options are News in Slow French, Italian, and German, and they have two versions (Spain, Latino) in Spanish.

Ideally, this is a tool we use *after* we have already established global relationships. Learning about world affairs can seem foreign in more ways than one; if we make connections *first*, then the news becomes more personal. And when it affects someone we know, we're more apt to take action to improve conditions around the world.

Equity in NIS

This website offers a seven-day trial period, but unfortunately, it does not offer a free, "tier 1" subscription. I recommend planning a unit, project, or lesson for this tool, and implementing it during a seven-day trial. In order to have increased access after that seven-day period, however, you can ask the school to do a trial as well. Perhaps the media specialist could set that up, and that would give you a total of 14 days of free access. After that, it's $19.99/month.

NIS has a couple features that are excellent for supporting different types of learners as well. First, they offer *leveled* news—Beginner, Intermediate, and Advanced—so teachers can use this resource across the levels or within the same class, supporting different language levels. (Note: At this time, the German version only offers Beginner and Intermediate levels.)

Second, within the different levels of language, students can choose the *speed* at which they hear the news. This gives students further choice to meet needs.

Third, all of the languages offer several "Series." They include a range of topics, but one of them that is consistent among the languages is guided meditation in the target language. These could pair nicely with a health topics unit, but they also could simply be a healthy tool to regularly use in class, particularly in light of widespread mental health issues in students. Similar guided meditations can be found on YouTube as well, but they're not necessarily geared toward language learners or educational settings.

Tying NIS to Global Education Principles

In particular, this resource aids students in **Recognizing Perspectives**. The most interesting and educational piece arrives when students compare and analyze how the same news is presented in different parts of the target language-speaking world. *How are they similar? How are they different? What about the contexts of these cultures might make the views different? Is this story told where I'm living now? If not, why not? If so, how does it compare?*

Educator Spotlight: Shauna Anderson
Position: French Teacher
School: Polaris Expeditionary School
City, State: Fort Collins, CO

How have you used News in Slow French in your classroom?

I have used News in Slow French as a reading and listening tool to facilitate culture and current event lessons in my French classroom. Students select the recent news video/article of interest to them (politics, climate, how to use a restroom in France, space, gastronomy, etc.), and they read along with the script at the speed (slow, super slow, etc.) they choose. They can hover over any difficult vocabulary, which is then defined in English.

In what ways could this be adapted for different levels (elementary, middle, high school, postsecondary.... or novice, intermediate, advanced)?

The options vary depending on the proficiency level and adapting from novice to advanced is easily accomplished by selecting those categories and then listening at a pace conducive to their abilities.

When using News in Slow French, is there anything students have noticed or shared that stood out to you?

Yes, they are able to print up the script/articles and use that as a resource if they need a break from their computer screens. This way, they can look up any unknown vocabulary on their own and fill it in on their script. I like to use this as a speaking/reading tool as well. We will popcorn read in groups, and it's a nice change of pace from using the computer screen to read.

How does News in Slow French support students' language development?

News in Slow French aids in reinforcing reading and listening skills. The news articles are current, important, cultural, and with a wide variety of selections. Students of all interests can easily find a topic they are passionate about which is a super sneaky and awesome way to trick them into also learning French because they are reading articles THEY care about!

How does reading the news support increased global competence in students?

Being aware of the current events in other countries and the conflicts and celebrations happening abroad is crucial to developing 21st-century critical thinking skills and postsecondary readiness in our world language classrooms. Having relevant global news articles available to world language students is an excellent tool to help students develop insight into the nature of language and culture in order to interact with cultural competence, which is one of our five world language "C's." In addition, reading the news builds connections for students, and my hope is that it sparks the desire to travel and explore our world, thanks to the gift of language.

15

Sustainable Development Goal Units

A few years into a new school in a new state, my district started the transition away from textbooks in world languages. For the most part, it became up to the individual teachers how to deliver the content; in other words, as long as we met the standards and had data to track growth, we had a significant amount of classroom autonomy. Some teachers continued to use the textbooks, while others shifted.

I recognize that for some, this is a nightmare; for others, it's a dream come true. Fortunately for me, when this happened, I had a significant number of years under my belt. I had taught high school French using four different textbook series, and I felt that none of them were perfect. I also felt strongly that I could create my own scope and sequence that would meet standards and logically support students' growth in language, so I was excited about this development!

I embarked on a multiyear implementation journey to reorganize my curriculum throughout each level of French, and I decided to use the SDGs as guideposts. The process isn't quick, but it starts with, of all things, butcher block paper.

My first step was making a map of my entire curriculum the way it looked at the time. Every unit and everything I covered was all mapped out by hand on butcher paper so I could see it all at once.

Because my upper-level class was International Baccalaureate, I stuck to mapping only levels 1–3, each on a separate sheet.

Next, I mapped out all 17 SDGs on a different sheet of butcher paper. Then I sat in the middle of all of my giant sheets of paper and began the reorganization process. My map looked like Table 15.1 to start.

To me, it didn't matter which SDGs came up in what level. I felt they were all appropriate for every level. Since that wasn't a factor, I simply started matching up SDGs to content I wanted to cover. The map evolved into Table 15.2.

TABLE 15.1 Skeleton for SDG Mapping

SDG:
Country/ies of Focus:
Vocab:
Grammar:
Verbs:
Project:
Novel and/or Film:

TABLE 15.2 Example of a FullyMapped SDG Unit in French

SDG #4: Quality Education
Country/ies of Focus: France, Canada, Switzerland, Belgium, Cameroon, French Polynesia
Vocab:
school supplies (review from previous unit)
school classes (new)
telling time (new)
days of the week (review)
descriptions (review from previous unit)
Grammar:
oui vs. si (review + new)
the near future (new)
interrogative adjectives (some review, some new)
Verbs:
to have (review from previous unit)
to go (new)
Project:
school skit
Novel and/or Film:
Jean-Paul et ses bonnes idées (novel)
Au Revoir les Enfants (classic film)

This structure allowed me to teach how I saw fit for my students, and it permitted different methods of teaching and learning. For example, I approach some concepts from the ground up, explicitly teaching those grammatical structures; on the other hand, I also teach some concepts in the exact opposite way, presenting students with fully formed structures and not breaking them down until later.

Integrating the SDGs into world language units works with any method or style of teaching and learning. They can be woven into a textbook-based environment or guide a textbook-free format. SDG #2, No Hunger, works well with any unit that includes food, and that same unit could include SDG #6, Clean Water and Sanitation. SDG #5, Gender Equality, pairs well with a unit that includes sports and activities, while SDG #8, Good Jobs and Economic Growth, lends itself well to a unit that includes professions and focuses on the future.

Equity in SDG Units

Framing units with the SDGs—either units we create from scratch or those made for us—*aid* in establishing a global approach to the curriculum, though, ultimately, the responsibility is ours. When we take steps to create a more global view of our content, more of our students will be able to see themselves, their families, and their histories in their education.

Tying SDG Units to Global Education Principles

The Asia Society's framework quadrants (Investigate the World, Recognize Perspectives, Communicate Ideas, and Take Action) are bound together by disciplinary and interdisciplinary study. The SDGs are an efficient way of delivering interdisciplinary content, as every discipline can create ties to the SDGs. The SDGs, therefore, can act as a guide and a common thread, tying the framework quadrants together.

SECTION 3
Leveraging Higher-Cost Options

16

Student Trips Abroad

I teach in a high school, and it's not uncommon for students to ask me if they can "friend" me on social media after they graduate. "After you turn 21, you are free to friend request me on Facebook," I say. (This immediately rules out many because—giggle, giggle—"No one uses Facebook, Madame.")

Some reply with "What? Why? But we officially won't be your students anymore after we graduate, so why make us wait?"

"Because I have no desire to see any photos or read any comments about anything that happens on your 21st birthday! I'm *grown!* My Facebook feed has *standards!*" I joke.

"Oh. That's fair."

As it turns out, many *do* send me a Facebook friend request after they turn 21, and it has been wonderful to see what my students are doing as adults. I especially enjoy seeing photos as they travel and experience the world.

One former student, Leah, grew into a prolific traveler who often posts photos from her trips. I commented on one of her pictures at one point, and her reply (Figure 16.1) stopped me in my tracks.

What Leah wrote was something I don't remember her expressing *while* traveling. I do remember her very clearly being giddy about finding a (way-too-expensive) Lord of the Rings piece of jewelry in a tiny tourist shop in Assisi, Italy, but I don't

DOI: 10.4324/9781003384267-19

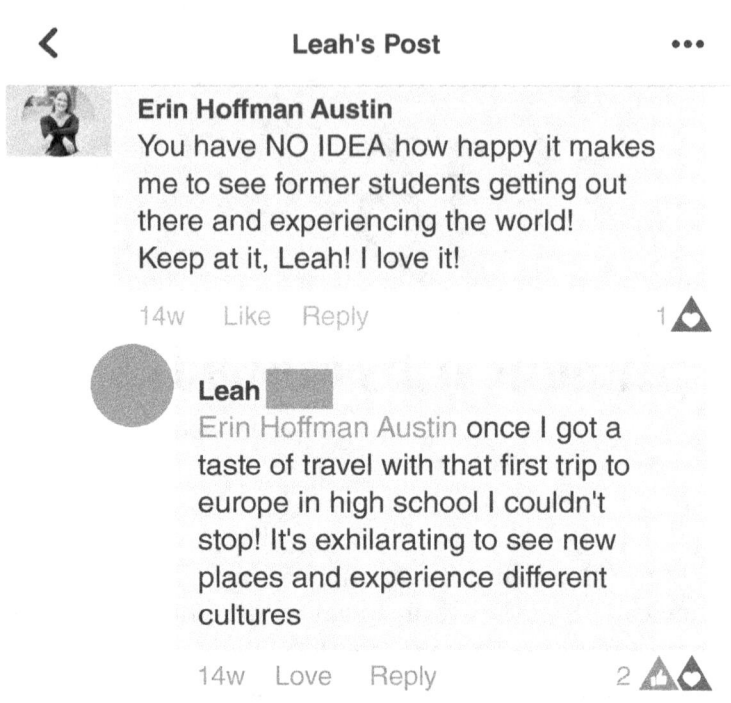

FIGURE 16.1 Social media post from a former student

remember her commenting on the culture or the location. Yet, years later, there I was finding out that our trip *did* change her and *did* shape the person she became. I keep a screenshot of that exchange in my Favorites folder on my phone so that I can remind myself of the power of student travel with just a couple clicks.

Organizing student travel is not for the faint of heart. It takes work, organization, persistence, and a willingness to go above and beyond what our contract requires. For anyone new to student travel, the easiest point of entry is to seek out a student travel company to partner with. These companies plan the itinerary, provide local guides and/or tour directors, book everything, take on liability, and more!

One of the simplest means for a curious teacher to learn about taking students abroad is to be the co-leader on another teacher's trip. Apprenticing under an experienced group leader will support a new leader in learning the ins and outs of the process in a way that is specific to their educational context.

There are, however, schools and districts that don't have a history of student travel, so in those contexts, there may not be a colleague from which we can learn the student travel ropes. Fortunately, some student travel companies, such as Education First (EF), will send first-time group leaders on a training tour to support these teachers in feeling confident in their ability to lead students in a foreign country. This (almost) all-expenses-paid training tour will take teachers to another country for four to six days, and participants can receive professional development hours for the workshops they attend. The workshops and the trip itself are designed to help you learn what a student tour feels like—what you do, what you see, what you eat, where you stay, the pace of the program—and to support you in pitching a trip to your school/district, getting it approved, and regularly getting students signed up.

Equity in Student Trips

The price tag of a student trip is the biggest barrier to students and families, and as much as I believe in the power of travel, I understand how difficult it can be. Too often, teachers think, "It's expensive, and there isn't much I can do about that because the student travel company sets the price." True, we can't often alter the price—or at least not significantly—but there are strategies to make the trips more financially accessible.

A simple way to alter the cost of your student trips is by varying the time of year, location, and length of trip. A Spanish teacher, for instance, could offer a four- or five-day trip to Mexico for a significantly lower cost to students than a ten-day trip to Spain. Furthermore, a spring break trip is always less expensive than a summer trip. It's worth considering a rotation of trips—alternating spring break with summer and alternating locations—to make it more equitable for students and families.

Varying the location has another effect as well: It offers a better representation of the target language-speaking world. French teachers, for example, could create a rotation with a variety of countries and continents. Language & Friendship (from Chapter 3) offers an excellent trip to Martinique which could be a spring break trip (lower cost) on a rotation with a Canadian and a European trip. Despite a positively glacial pace, there *are* travel companies expanding into francophone Africa with trips to Morocco and Senegal. Without words, this shows students that the francophone world spans multiple continents and isn't reserved to a predominantly white setting.

Most teachers are familiar with a common and highly *active* way of lowering the price of travel: fundraising. Either we have sold "premium" wrapping paper, chocolate, or frozen baked goods or we know someone who has. If this is what works for you and your context, by all means, keep doing it! For many, though, the time spent isn't equal to the reward.

One of the most powerful steps we can take as a teacher that has one of the most significant impacts on students is to offer a full scholarship for a trip abroad. The best part is that it's not as difficult as it may seem!

My favorite way to offer a full scholarship is directly through the student travel company. This makes it quick and easy for the teacher. Student travel companies all offer one free leader spot per X number of paying travelers. Let's use a "magic formula" of *six* paying travelers equals *one* trip leader traveling free as our example. This makes it easy to shoot for a trip with 18 student travelers. (In reality, I recommend aiming for 20 paying students instead of 18 because there is often at least one student who has to drop out prior to the trip.) The first six paying travelers cover the cost of one leader: you! The second six paying travelers cover the cost of your co-leader. The last six paying travelers cover a third leader, but in my view, it's not needed. Two competent adults can easily manage and lead 18 students, and often, three leaders can contribute to a "too many cooks in the kitchen" situation. Therefore, instead of covering the cost of an additional leader, the final six paying students cover the cost of a full scholarship for a student! Travel companies can quite easily make this happen, and typically the scholarship recipient will only need to cover passport fees, certain meals, and spending money.

Another option is raising the funds for a full scholarship through microdonations. These could be secured through a fundraising platform (e.g., GoFundMe, DonorsChoose) or through a specific platform your school uses for payments and accounts.

If a language department or teacher says, "The Italian classes are collecting donations to fund a full scholarship for one lucky student to travel on the school trip to Italy," many families will read that and automatically dismiss it, thinking, "We can't afford to donate." Too often, when the ask isn't specific, families *assume* they can't be part of it and *assume* that everyone who donates is donating a lot. But if we instead say, "We have a $1 donation campaign to raise money to fund a full scholarship for one lucky student! The goal is for every family in our school community to donate just $1 to our fund!" then the tables have turned. Instead of feeling *excluded*, families can feel *included*. Most (though not all) families could afford $1, and many, of course, will give far more. By setting the ask at a *low* amount while shooting for *high* participation, we include more families and make the fund a team effort. The donations raised can support a student scholarship, but the effort shouldn't be limited solely to the school. Reach out to the surrounding community with news of the $1 fundraising campaign! Journalists might be looking for an interesting and inspiring education story to promote in a newspaper, and houses of worship may be eager to support youth as well.

There are a multiple ways to select the full scholarship recipient. Some teachers or departments might require an application with short answer, essay, and/or interview components. The scholarship could be need-based, merit-based, or a combination of both. Or you could make it simple and draw a name. Choose what's best for your context and your students.

This chapter contains *two* spotlights: an Educator Spotlight and a Former Student Spotlight. The educator is an immigrant who regularly takes students back to his country of origin. The former student was a recipient of a full scholarship (as described in this chapter), and she shares her experience of a trip to Paris and Barcelona when she was in high school.

Tying Student Trips to Global Education Principles

Student trips are among the most profound methods of supporting students in **Investigating the World** beyond their immediate environment. Free time, in particular, allows a traveler to be less of an observer, like on a museum tour, and more of an active participant in the investigation. It is during free time that students venture out and take (what is often) their first steps in communicating and interacting with locals.

If the trip includes a family stay component, that makes it easier for students to **Recognize Perspectives** and **Communicate Ideas**. Much of this happens over meals with the host family, as the rest of the world so often takes pleasure in eating and in family time in a different—and lengthier—way than we typically experience in the United States. As students and the host families become increasingly comfortable with each other, more communication takes place. It becomes less about simply taking turns talking and more about interacting with each other: asking questions, probing deeper, and seeking to understand.

Although most trips don't include a **Take Action** element, there are some student travel companies, including EF Tours, that are expanding their repertoire of service-based trips. But often, the **Take Action** component that comes out of student travel is that a seed is planted. As with my experience with Leah, leaders of a middle or high school student trip, in particular, don't always see how a student trip spurs *action* or a mindset development in the student. We simply have to trust that it *will*.

Educator Spotlight: Nico C. Henry
Position: French Teacher
School: Fossil Ridge High School
City, State: Fort Collins, CO

Taking high school students abroad is a lot of work. Why do you choose to do it?

I decided to take my students to France because I wanted to share the culture that I was born into with them. I do believe that immersion is the best way to not only start to learn a language but also appreciate the various cultures in which this language is spoken. In my case, being born and raised in France, I was, and still am, very much attached to my culture. For my personal experience, immigrating to the United States was a huge step, but I quickly decided that in order to embrace American culture, I had to not only force myself to learn the language well but also learn about its culture.

There are teachers who are worried about taking that first student trip. What would you say to them as encouragement?

Indeed, it is a huge step and a very scary one, nonetheless. I would first recommend checking with people who have led trips in the past and to seek their input. For example, the company they used, how to choose your chaperones (choose carefully) and students (maybe even have an application process), the legitimacy of the cost, and maybe pairing with someone who has done it before. But most importantly, it is a fun and rewarding experience to take students abroad. And you will likely be surprised by their reactions and positive behaviors—things you might not have expected. In some instances, you discover the true nature of your students. It gets easier with every trip.

What are some observations you've had of your students while abroad? How are they different? What jumps out at you about their experience?

I think that in the setting of the classroom, some students might seem detached or uninterested, yet still present and turning in work and getting a good grade. But once abroad, you see them in awe in front of a sculpture, painting, or building; they come to you to discuss things they have seen or to share their excitement about what they've seen. You could also have a shy student in the classroom who suddenly starts chatting with a waiter at a French restaurant or a baker, enjoying themselves, taking risks you would never suspect. Also, I have been surprised to see how well students form a cohesive group—the popular kids reaching out to the shy kids and including them in the group dynamic.

Travel abroad is expensive. Are there methods that you have used, or that you have known others who have used, to increase access to the experience?

I have not personally used any methods yet, but I am strongly considering organizing fundraisers with local restaurants in the future, just to help my students a little bit. Otherwise, I have been trying to advise families and students by explaining that the cost of the trip can be divided into monthly payments (i.e., the cost of a car payment). It is important to plan the trip well in advance (two years) so the families have more time to pay for the trip. I advise my students to speak to their parents often and to propose that the cost of the trip could be shared if the students could find a part-time job because the trips can be so costly.

What are some tips you would give teachers looking to establish a regular travel abroad program at their school?

Have a consistent travel schedule; for example, we go every two years during spring break. That way, students know when the next trip is coming up. Try to stay with the same company, and make a connection with the travel advisor of the company. Make connections with the people abroad as well in order to improve future experiences—like the tour director, the restaurants, and the bus driver. Having a good tour director is of paramount importance. Find one you like and request that person every time. Try to keep your trips private so you don't have to share with another school. I have personally never traveled with another school, but I feel that the extra cost is worth it to not risk traveling with students or teachers whom you don't know and may not have the same behavioral standards as you.

How does establishing a tradition of taking students abroad support increased global competence in students?

We've had students deciding to study abroad or continue with the language in high school or after. The trips abroad have been a gigantic inspiration to students, opening minds and eyes. Not everything can be gained from the internet; a true, real-life experience is irreplaceable. This helps build a tradition, for example, having siblings wanting to take a trip like their big brothers or sisters took. Also, this establishes a relationship with parents, knowing they can trust me with their children on a trip abroad.

Former Student Spotlight: Magali Torres
City, State: Burnsville, MN

How old were you when you traveled to Paris and Barcelona? At the time, what languages did you speak, and at what level?

I was 17 years old when I traveled to Paris and Barcelona. I spoke English, Spanish, and intermediate French.

What did it mean to you to receive a full scholarship to travel to Paris and Barcelona as a high school student? How did it feel when you found out you were going?

Growing up, I always saw movies that were filmed in France and I always used to say, "That will be me someday." However, I never actually thought I would ever have the opportunity to go to Europe. I remember my Big Sister (Big Brothers Big Sisters) sat me down with my mom and told me she was giving me a scholarship to go to Europe with her and her students. I had to process it for the first month because I couldn't believe it. It was the most exciting feeling. I felt extremely lucky to have been given this opportunity.

How did travel enhance what you were learning in school?

Traveling enhanced my confidence. I grew up being extremely shy. However, being placed with a group of students I had never met before and speaking a language that I wasn't fully comfortable with made me step outside my "comfort zone." I learned two new cultures I had never been exposed to before, and I learned the different foods that were customary in both countries.

What do you remember most, either linguistically or culturally, about your experience abroad?

What I remember most about France and Spain are the cultural similarities to my Mexican culture. The amount of respect that is given to someone else is very important in my culture, and I saw that it was similar, in both the French and Spanish cultures. They value food and family time as much as we do. It was exciting to know our cultures were similar in some ways that I wouldn't be able to relate to an American culture.

How have travel experiences—of all kinds—shaped who you are today?

Travel experiences have transformed my way of thinking about life. I have learned to be more empathetic toward others and appreciate the differences between me and others around me. Living in a city that has a lot of diversity, I have been able to adapt quicker and respect other people's traditions. I am more aware of how I compose myself and interact with others.

How does travel abroad increase global competence in students?

Traveling abroad increases a student's critical thinking skills. In today's world, a lot of employers are looking for someone who is able to adapt to changes and is able to problem solve. Traveling teaches us how to problem solve when we don't speak the language or are lost in a place we have never been before. Students play an important role in improving and strengthening our society, and traveling will help change their perspective toward certain topics and teach them to become more empathetic to others.

17

Concordia Language Villages

For many U.S. American adults, we can pinpoint exact times in which we felt, or even said out loud, "We're not in Kansas anymore" when we ventured to new areas of the United States. Ruby slippers and wicked witches aside, we felt like Dorothy in *The Wizard of Oz*. We knew we changed locations—we could see it and feel it—but it didn't make 100% sense because we were still in our home country.

That describes the feeling youth and adults experience at a Concordia Language Villages (CLV) camp in the north lakes and woods of Minnesota. It *feels* like you're in a foreign country: The language is different, the food is different, and, other than the surroundings, the culture is distinctly not Minnesotan.

Established in 1961, this nonprofit's mission is "to inspire courageous global citizens," and although their youth camps are the most well known, they also offer language enrichment and training for adults and families. As of this publication, Concordia offers programming in 15 different languages: Arabic, Chinese, Danish, English, Finnish, French, German, Italian, Japanese, Korean, Norwegian, Portuguese, Russian, Spanish, and Swedish.

Youth camps range from family weekends (supporting our youngest, preschool learners) to one- to four-week intensives. From the moment students arrive, full reliance on the target language is necessary. The leaders of the camps are typically native or heritage speakers who are highly skilled in engaging students in comprehensible language use and activities. Students leave camp with a "local is global" experience that is unparalleled, attracting language learners from all over the country and from all walks of life. President and First Lady Clinton even visited the camps because their daughter, Chelsea, attended the German camp for six summers in the 1990s.

Equity in CLV

The fact that the language camps at Concordia provide a linguistic and cultural immersion experience that doesn't require a crossing an ocean makes them the perfect addition to a student travel program. A weekend or summer trip to CLV fits nicely into a student trip rotation, and with a lower price point than a trip abroad, it opens the rich experience to more students.

Students can also take advantage of CLV's scholarship program. Because of an established tradition of excellence spanning multiple decades, CLV has maintained enthusiastic support from a lengthy list of donors. Their Passport Fund regularly provides need-based scholarships, and students are encouraged to apply.

With high-quality curriculum and an impressive track record, Concordia's high school credit programs are an exceptional choice for students. These programs can support students looking to advance more quickly through the language choices at their schools or students who are drawn to a language that their school doesn't offer. CLV makes an equitable choice in making credit programs available via residential summer programs and in virtual programs during the school year. This also supports students who may have a scheduling conflict: They want to take a language class and another class that are only offered during the same period.

The fact that CLV supports the learning of over a dozen world languages is another reason to celebrate their prowess in the field of world language education. Few universities can boast that kind of depth and breadth! The CLV languages span multiple continents, and they vary from high numbers of native speakers (e.g., Chinese, English) to smaller numbers of native speakers (e.g., Danish, Finnish). This allows students a greater amount of choice in language than they can find in nearly all schools. World language teachers know that when students are interested in the language they're studying, learning is accelerated and longer-lasting. *All* languages can open the world to students and increase global competence, so exposure to choice in language opens the door to more students.

Tying CLV to Global Education Principles

In particular, CLV is adept at building students' capacity to **Communicate Ideas**. This starts small, often by teaching language learners with little-to-no experience how to communicate needs and wants in a camp environment effectively. This lays the groundwork for what is to come later: communicating bigger picture ideas and topics of global significance in more than one language.

Educator Spotlight: Chris Littmann
Position: German Teacher
School: Minnetonka School District
City, State: Minnetonka, MN

What is your involvement with CLV?

For 16 years, I have been taking groups of students to Waldsee (CLV's German camp) for their weekend programs.

How is the experience at CLV special?

It is special because it is real. I feel the environment changes as you drive through the woods, and when you get that first glimpse of the "Bahnhof," you believe this could really be Germany. Everything from the food to the music to the activities is very authentic and fun.

What is a typical day like at Waldsee for students? For teachers?

For the weekend program, Saturday is the most impactful day. Students gather in their cabins at about 8:00 am before walking over to breakfast. After that, they travel in small groups through a series of stations. Every year there is a different theme to which the stations align. At one station, students may use shapes and colors when learning about Paul Klee. At another, they may learn vocabulary such as twigs, needles, leaves, and pinecones when given the task to build a miniature hut using only what they can find in the woods.

After two hours, students gather back for a snack then they have choice activities. Depending on the season, there are several options such as soccer or volleyball (even more fun when they do it in the snow), baking cookies, painting signs, relaxing in the sauna, playing in a Foosball tournament, or learning a new board game. All of the stations and activities are guided in the target language.

At about 1:00 they come back together for lunch. At mealtime there is always playful interaction and language—lots of language.

After lunch, students continue with the remaining stations and gather for large-group singing and dancing and snack, and then another round of choice activities. It is now late afternoon and students return to their cabins for a short pause and some time to change for the evening banquet. This is a fabulous three-course meal with awards and acknowledgments followed by music and dancing.

As a teacher, I am not given any assignments or duties; however, I choose to participate in almost everything. I start the day in the cabin lounge area having simple conversations with the students. I often run around to all of the stations, taking pictures and engaging with the students as they participate. During choice activities, I sometimes join in, or I use this time to collaborate with other German teachers. It is wonderful to share ideas over a cup of tea and make new friends in our profession. I do sit with students during meals and talk with them as much as possible, but the counselors on-site do a fantastic job of managing the program and keeping the students engaged all day.

Why do you choose CLV as an activity to add to your German program?

I teach Level I German, and most students have not yet had an international experience. CLV provides a truly authentic adventure and opens their minds to a different culture. I also find it valuable for students' self-confidence; they feel great as they realize, even after only a few months in the classroom, that they have learned enough German to really communicate and complete tasks.

How does involvement as a "camper" at a CLV support increased global competence in students?

Nobody questions how or why something is the way it is when we are at Waldsee. Students just accept that this is how we do things here. If this is their first exposure to global differences, I believe it is positive and will impact how they perceive future moments.

18

Global Literature

All was well. Those were the last words in book seven of J.K. Rowling's *Harry Potter* series, and although all was apparently well for Harry, it certainly wasn't for me. Coming to the end of a series my family and I loved so much and an end to characters that had been brought to life by brilliant writing ushered in real sadness. I felt a true *loss*. Strangely (or not?), many people I know expressed precisely the same feeling upon reading those final three words.

Why do I bring this up? What does *Harry Potter* have to do with world language education? Because this series, for so many people, young and old, made an indelible impact on its readers. Fantastic writing and compelling stories have a unique power to do that. They can make students *feel*. And dream. And question. And create. And love.

And laugh and cry in the same sentence. Enter: *Oscar et la dame rose* (Oscar and the Pink Lady). This book is the story of a fictional, ten-year-old boy's life…a boy who is in the hospital, dying of cancer. The entire book is written as letters that Oscar writes to a god he's not even sure exists, but his volunteer health aide, Mamie Rose, the "pink lady," suggests it as an exercise to process his feelings. This little boy is *hilarious*—and has a bit of a potty mouth—but he's also grappling with true life and death issues.

In a single sentence, he could say something funny followed by something that makes your heart physically ache.

At the end of the book, predictably, Oscar dies. My upper-level French students struggle with it. They grow attached to him and, being American, they hope for a big Hollywood rescue at the end. But as they process grief—and some do cry—I point something out to them, saying, "Isn't it fantastic that you can feel this deeply *in your non-native language?*" At that, they perk up. *Yes, that is pretty fantastic.*

Classroom literature can profoundly impact students. To expand our students' views and worlds, and to speak directly to their minds and hearts, one step is to adopt literature from a selection of countries or regions of your target language at a variety of proficiency levels. In particular, when we choose authors who were raised in the culture featured in their stories, it becomes a superb way to learn *from* the world.

The word *variety* is key. We can specifically use literature to highlight diverse perspectives, both inter- and intra-cultural. Then when we discuss those perspectives, we cannot leave out the crucial question of *why?* Why does the main character feel X? Why do I feel the same or different? What, in our respective histories, contributed to our views?

As we guide our students in these (sometimes difficult) conversations, it can be tempting for students to want a solution. Something clear-cut and final that wraps up an issue or theme as right or wrong. But empathy and knowledge aren't born solely out of certainty. Empathy, I would argue, is more deeply born in the struggle. Wrestling with a concept, feeling compelled to discuss, and searching for more information and perspectives all contribute to the growth of a global mindset.

Equity in Global Literature

As we select literature for our curriculums, there are factors to consider before clicking "add to cart." It may be most appropriate to start with what literature you already have and that you and the students typically enjoy. From there, take a look at who the protagonists are. Is there diversity in whose stories are centered? Do the stories feature main characters of different genders, family structures, life experiences, and perceived race, to name a few?

Second, ask those same questions again, but this time, direct them at the authors. Be wary of a classroom library whose authors are exclusively white Americans because that isn't at all representative of the global reach of our languages and the writers who hail from a wealth of countries.

Third, consider location. Where do the stories take place? One country or context or many, spanning our target language lands? As world language teachers, we may *personally* play favorites with countries or cities in our target language cultures, but students often do not. Our job is not to teach *our* favorites but to support students in discovering *their own*.

Cost can rear its ugly, prohibitive head as we work to grow classroom libraries that are equitable and that inspire. The NEA Foundation is a champion of global education and of equity. They continually offer grants for educators who are striving to innovate with global education and equity-based strategies. Check out their website (in the Resources section) for the most up-to-date grants, and then apply! These grants offer up big dollars, and big dollars can equal big developments for growth in world language classrooms.

No time to write a grant? Check out Global Storybooks! It's an online treasure trove of stories, and teachers can search by target language or by country. This site is uniquely well suited to different learning preferences and proficiency levels because students can listen to the stories and slow down the speed, and teachers can print the stories as a PDF and do scaffolded activities with the text.

Tying Global Literature to Global Education Principles

Global literature supports students in **Investigating the World** and **Recognizing Perspectives**. This is particularly true when the literature is well written, well selected, and supported by strong lessons created by the teacher. Firsthand accounts and personal narratives can be uniquely powerful stories that can transform minds and hearts and strengthen the growth of empathetic learners and citizens.

Teachers can take the stories' messages a step further by inviting the author to speak to their class (in person or virtually). We may not always get a "yes," and some of the positive replies may come with a sticker price or a schedule that makes it prohibitive, but it never hurts to ask. Many authors are happy to jump on a video chat to answer a couple questions for free, and when this happens, the stories come alive even more. If level-appropriate, the questions and the replies should be in the target language. This also helps students **Communicate Ideas** with diverse audiences.

Educator Spotlight: Tamara Ramirez-Torres
Position: Spanish and Reading Teacher for Newcomers to the United States
School: El Colegio High School
City, State: Minneapolis, MN

What does a more global approach in the readers and novels that you use in class mean to you as a teacher?

As a teacher to newcomers to this country, it is important first to celebrate their home countries, and second, to teach and celebrate the cultures of students and communities that are not necessarily in our school, but around their neighborhoods.

What might using a global approach in the readers and novels that you use in class mean to students?

It means that they have the opportunity to learn from the cultures and struggles of other communities that, like them, came to the United States to find safety and better life opportunities.

When selecting readers/novels to use in class, what should other teachers specifically look for?

In my experience from the various book clubs that I have been in, I can't really tell you what other teachers should look for because I still see a lot of biases and, sadly, some discrimination in our conversations.

Teachers are afraid of teaching certain books because they are afraid of the reactions from parents and/or administrators. I personally look for ways to teach students cultural differences, geography, current events, and historical facts, and all while enjoying these amazing books.

I think teachers should teach books looking through the globalization lens in order to be able to talk to parents and administrators about why these books are important.

Conversely, what should other teachers seek to <u>avoid</u> when selecting readers/novels to use in class?

I can only speak for myself, but I look for positive outcomes, acceptance, lessons taught and learned, resilience, looking at situations through different lenses, historical facts, and great young characters.

How does establishing a more global literature component to a class support increased global competence in students?

- Students will be exposed to rich literature that will open their eyes to what is happening in the different cultures and countries of their peers and the struggles they have faced.
- They will be able to understand why different communities look for help and asylum in our country.
- They will learn what is happening with local and statewide policies that can help or destroy these communities.
- They will learn that these communities are not very different from them, just from another country.
- They will learn, and possibly enjoy, what these different cultures have to offer us.

Are there specific readers/novels that support a global view that you especially recommend and like? Include title, author, and any topics that can easily pair with the book.

Where to start! These are a couple of the books I have read in my classes both in Spanish and in English. I have used all of these in my high school classes. These titles have been read in many book clubs I've been a part of, and I am proud to say that I have read most of them in my class—some in student book clubs and others used as reference.

These are all amazing books that our students should be exposed to. It is also good to read books to which our students can relate and see people like them and their countries portrayed accurately. I have been able to learn about so many amazing countries and communities and pass this knowledge and wonderful books to my students. There are so many more wonderful books (and themes) to explore!

- *Welcome to the New World* by Jake Halpern (refugees, the struggle to fit in)
- *When We Were Alone* by David A. Robertson (resilience, family)
- *Go Show the World* by Wab Kinew (Indigenous heroes)
- *Refugee* by Alan Gratz (refugees, resilience, family, struggles)
- *Borders* by Thomas King (resilience, pride in who you are)
- *The Color of My Words* by Lynn Joseph (resistance, resilience, dreams)
- *Hector* by Adrienne Wright (resistance, change, resilience)
- *Patron Saints of Nothing* by Randy Ribay (family, resilience, faith, struggle to reconcile grief and guilt)
- *Nour's Secret Library* by Wafa' Tarnowska (resilience, coping with war, disaster, despair, community)
- *Home Is Not a Country* by Safia Elhillo (understanding and honoring your home culture, yearning to fit in)
- *Strong as Fire, Fierce as Flame* by Supriya Kelkar (taking control of your destiny, resilience, self-worth, resistance)
- *It Ain't So Awful, Falafel* by Firoozeh Dumas (fitting in when one's country is at war with the country you live in, resilience, resistance)

19

Global Volunteers and Global Leaders

My senior year of college I had what I assume is a normal reaction to nearly being finished: a "But should I do something *amazing* before entering the working world of adults?" type of freak out. I had known that I was going to teach for as long as I could remember, and I although I was sure of that path, there was also something in me that longed for an adventure before making teaching official. I was leaning toward the Peace Corps.

Leaving the country on a mission to make the world better sounded wonderful, but I wrestled with it. It was, after all, a major decision and a significant deviation from The Plan. Ultimately, what kept me in the country was the length of the Peace Corps commitment pitted against my mounting student loans and my desire to pay them off as soon as possible.

I couldn't shake that feeling of wanting to do a program similar to the Peace Corps, however, and shortly after graduating I found a worthy solution: Global Volunteers. The fact that the organization was non-government-affiliated *and* non-religiously-affiliated was attractive to me. I also appreciated that I had options all over the world, ranging from one- to three-week programs. Although I didn't realize it at the time, the most important aspect of the organization is that it was the locals—*not* someone in an office in the United States—planning and overseeing the work.

I ultimately participated in two programs in separate years; the first was in Quito, Ecuador. There, I spent all day, every day, at Camp Hope. It was part orphanage, part school, part medical center, and part daycare center. Many of the children who attended Camp Hope had significant physical and/or mental disabilities. Our program director explained that this is an extremely common problem in Ecuador and largely a result of lack of prenatal care and proper nutrition for expectant mothers. All of the children there came from families in substantial poverty.

Each day, we would arrive at Camp Hope and receive our assignments. For some, it was construction on new parts of the center. For the doctors in the group, it was medical care. (Much of the medical care was giving birth control and the accompanying education to women who came to the center.) I often worked in a small team of volunteers, giving English lessons to incredibly bright and fun children, all elementary school-aged. All of us in the Global Volunteer group would, at some point in the day, simply spend time playing with children and helping those who needed help eating during meal times.

Some members of my group spoke Spanish, and some did not. Of course, the trial-by-fire approach was great fun for me as a language teacher! I left with more Spanish than when I arrived...but as a French teacher, those R sounds tripped me up every time!

Here is an excerpt from my journal from this service trip in August of 2007:

I have always known, on a superficial level, that the U.S. is the richest, most powerful country in the world, etc., etc. I don't think it was until today that I fully grasped what that means. I don't think I understood that, not because of my own merit, but simply because of where my mother gave birth, I am privileged. I came into this world with privileges that many in the world will never even see in adulthood.

Realizing that furthered my belief in the vision of a global community. A community in which we are all responsible for each other. A world whose citizens think of or pray for, work with, support and help each other.

My second service trip with Global Volunteers was in Salvador, Brazil. There, we worked at different work locations: Hospital Martagão Gesteira, Santa Casa, Hospital Santa Izabel, and NACCI. The first hospital was largely charity-based, serving those with low incomes, while the second was distinctly better kept and served those with health insurance. Santa Casa was a preschool for one- to six-year-olds, with two classrooms per age group. Again, it was for families with low incomes, and they had to apply for acceptance. NACCI was a residential facility for children who were temporarily in Salvador to receive treatment for cancer, primarily leukemia. If needed, the children's families could stay at NACCI too.

At all three locations, our main job was simply playing with the children who were receiving treatment. In other words, we were tasked with making the days a little brighter for children and families in an incredibly difficult situation. I spent hours upon hours playing Jenga, losing badly at Uno, and doing puzzles. At NACCI, the children called us "tia" and "tio" (Portuguese for "aunt" and "uncle", respectively), which melted all our hearts.

I attempted to learn some Portuguese before I went because *Eu não falo portugês,* but it turned out to be more difficult than I predicted, despite fluency in French and English and a rudimentary level of Spanish. Much of the communication was done with gesturing, but I did participate in a good deal of singing in Portuguese while at Santa Casa! There, we would sometimes assist teachers with classroom tasks, and other times we'd find ourselves participating in the activities right along with the children, helping to keep them on task and engaged.

Salvador helped me grow linguistically and culturally. I was able to see performances of Capoeira, the Brazilian half-dance/half-fight martial art, and the Balé Folklorico, each of which I found endlessly captivating. It's arguable that I learned the most about the culture at my first professional soccer game, and without a doubt, I learned the most colorful Portuguese vocabulary there too!

Both of my Global Volunteer experiences were life-changing in ways that were intensely beautiful *and* powerfully heartbreaking. I was grateful to be able to learn and serve under the guidance of empathetic and formidable adults committed to meaningful advancement of their people and city. Most significantly, I grew linguistically and increased my empathy and cultural knowledge.

Global Volunteers is largely set up for post-high school adults, although they do take families who want to volunteer together. I find the organization ripe for partnerships with universities. There could be powerful cross-curricular connections with world language majors and with students of another discipline, depending on the country and service area needs. For instance, Spanish majors and pre-med students would be the perfect combination for serving together in Quito.

The power of service is so extraordinary that I longed for a similar option for younger students...and then I came to know Global Leaders.

Global Leaders has a simple(-sounding), slogan-based mission: Students empowering students. Like Global Volunteers, they provide a service opportunity abroad—specifically, in Guatemala—but potentially the most integral part of their program takes place prior to the service trip. During the year leading up to take-off, students spend a year at home (Fort Collins, Colorado) undertaking service projects in the local community and participating in activities to build leadership capacity. When the *local* becomes *global*, the service and the leadership models continue. While in Guatemala, the students participate in locally-led service projects during the day, and at night, they stay with local families.

This organization is small and locally-based in northern Colorado, so why do I highlight it when it (comparatively) benefits so few? The program is streamlined and has a strong history. There's no reason individuals inspired by the model couldn't replicate it in their own cities. The international partnership could expand with Guatemala, or it could branch out into other countries.

Equity in Global Volunteers and Global Leaders

Importantly, both of these service-based organizations recognize that opportunities for service exist at home in the United States *and* abroad; in other words, "need" isn't exclusive to "others". This is a vital view to offer students.

Global Volunteers has programs in the U.S. and abroad, and the length of each of their programs varies. As with student travel (Chapter 16), this makes the cost and the calendar of programs vary, all of which leads to increased access for participation.

Global Leaders, as you will learn in this chapter's Educator Spotlight, works extensively with students and families to make the trips become a reality to anyone who wants to go. In addition to substantial financial support, which levels the playing field for interested students, Global Leaders' model also creates a more level community feel while abroad. Often, service programs unintentionally create lopsided power dynamics in the host countries with the people *serving* repeatedly hearing the narrative that they're "helping" those who are "less fortunate". This creates a power imbalance that perpetuates *sympathy* over *empathy* and may contribute to unconscious feelings of superiority in the program participants. Although it may seem simple, the fact that Global Leaders student travelers stay with Guatemalan families in their homes helps to decrease a false power narrative.

Relatedly, the fact that both Global Volunteers and Global Leaders are largely driven by local service needs and local leaders—as opposed to out-of-country, foreign plans, desires, and directors—is a hallmark of an ethical program. Moreover, Global Volunteers specifically employs the words "wherever we're *invited* to serve" in their literature, demonstrating that the volunteers are there via *invite* and as *guests*, not as local directors.

Tying Global Volunteers and Global Leaders to Global Education Principles

Ideally, participation in service programs such as these would be the result of acquiring knowledge: *I have learned, I have created a plan, and now I'm ready to* **Take Action**. It might be that the students **Investigate the World** prior to the service trips, but that will surely take place during the trips as well. Both types of trips factor in time for cultural exchange, and this supports the participants in **Recognizing Perspectives**.

Educator Spotlight: Joe Fontana
Position: Executive Director, Global Leaders (current); assistant principal (former)
School: Poudre High School
City, State: Fort Collins, CO

What is/was your involvement with Global Leaders?

I am the Co-Founder and Executive Director. I was a classroom teacher for 22 years and a school administrator for 7 years.

How does the experience Global Leaders provides help student participants grow their global competence?

Our program is a nine-month leadership training and service-learning adventure. Students are performing service-learning activities in their community for 8.5 months of the program. Most of the projects we participate in locally are student conceptualized, planned, and implemented. Our mission is a three-word mission: "Students Empowering Students". GL Students participate by doing! We follow the John Maxwell progression of: **Model** (Watch me!), **Mentor** (We work together; I'm 60% you're 40%), **Monitor** (We work together; y'all are 60% and I'm 40%), **Motivate** (Y'all do it, and I am here for support), and **MULTIPLY** (Y'all model for others, and multiply leadership). We expect nothing less than our students to become the leaders of their chosen fields.

There is always a concern about a "savior" mentality with organizations that bring American students or adults abroad. How does Global Leaders combat this? In other words, how does Global Leaders' set-up support true teaching and learning with the world in the spirit of service?

We have learned through the years that we are a "pair of hands" in all the communities in which we work. We collaborate with the communities to create projects they believe necessary for the betterment of their place. We consistently emphasize to our students and teachers that we are not needed; these communities will survive without us. We make every effort to live by the Lila Watson quote, *"If you have come to help me, you are wasting your time. But if you have come because your liberation is bound up with mine, then let us walk together"*. With all that said, we have made mistakes in this area. We consistently review our systems with our partners, and when we make mistakes we acknowledge them, fix them, and move forward.

How does Global Leaders support students who are interested in participating but don't have the financial resources to do so?

For 25 years, every student who has had a desire to be a part of our program has participated. We fundraise and write grants to be able to tell families, "If your kid wants to participate and is willing to work for it, we will make sure they can participate." We have never turned a kid away because of lack of finances. Another way students are able to defer program fee costs is to participate in our Work and Earn program. Students are paid to work in our office and assist with all aspects of our nonprofit from grant writing, lesson planning, conceptualizing, planning and implementing service-learning projects.

20
CIEE High School Summer Abroad

Eyes wide, a rapid, double blink, and a "Whoa!" That's what my students inevitably get from me when we reconnect in the fall after they experienced a CIEE High School Summer Abroad program. Their accent has changed, their air is a bit more "worldly," and they've become noticeably more linguistically confident.

Founded in 1947, CIEE is a nonprofit that facilitates cultural exchanges. In their own words,

> CIEE's mission is to **humanize international relations** and **foster peace** through international education and exchange programs that **promote intercultural understanding**.
>
> We strive to **increase global harmony and stability** by helping individuals learn to embrace people different from themselves and ideas different from their own.
>
> We **prepare future leaders** who will be able to communicate across cultures to tackle issues confronting our globally interconnected and multicultural world.

That mission and those actions feel directly lifted from a Global Education Playbook! In particular, note the focus on the future. This is an organization that isn't planning for today; instead, it envisions the kind of world global educators want to see and takes steps to ensure that vision becomes reality by investing in our youth who will take us there.

AFS is another well-known and reputable nonprofit organization with a similar structure and aim: *to provide intercultural learning opportunities to help people develop the knowledge, skills and understanding needed to create a more just and peaceful world.* While CIEE's power, in part, lies in its ability to provide full scholarships and in its vast summer offerings, the bread and butter of AFS are its semester, trimester, or academic year study abroad experiences for high school or gap year students. They, too, offer scholarships, and they have expanded to virtual exchanges and short exchanges called *AFS Academies.*

Equity in Study Abroad

3.4 million U.S. dollars. That's the amount of scholarship money CIEE has to dole out in the year of this book's publication. Whoa. An exceptionally generous, anonymous donor who believes in the power of global travel to support language learning gives millions to CIEE each year to be used in the form of both merit and need-based scholarships. Program applicants can apply for a scholarship, and within a couple of months, they find out what their scholarship offer is: none, partial, or full. They can accept the offer if it works for their family or turn it down if it does not. Students can easily turn down a scholarship and then apply again the next year, trying for a larger offer. Recently, one of my students spent a month living and studying in Paris on a full scholarship. A dream come true!

Teachers should take note of a couple of tips regarding the scholarships:

1. The donor has a special place in her heart for language-based programs. Applicants who put a language-based program in their top three choices are more likely to get a scholarship offer.

2   Spell-check, then revise, revise, and revise again. Better essays (there are three) equal a better chance at receiving a scholarship. I recommend setting up times to meet with applicants as a group. Teachers can do a round of essay feedback, but I've found that peer reviews on the essays are worth the time as well.

Although it doesn't offer a *significant* amount of flexibility, it's worth noting that CIEE does offer two different summer sessions for their programs. This helps students and families because more flexibility equals more access.

CIEE also makes a concerted effort to create programming that is appropriate for a range of interests in a range of locations. For example, students can choose a language, arts and culture, business, social change, or Science, Technology, Engineering, and Math-based program in Africa, Asia-Pacific, Europe, or Latin America. The program sites vary in culture, dominant religion, ethnicity, language, customs, and more, and this can support students in picking the right "home away from home."

Tying Study Abroad to Global Education Principles

Because the High School Summer Abroad program is education-based, particular attention is paid to the **Investigate the World** quadrant in the Asia Society's matrix. Most mornings in the language-based programs, for example, students are in classrooms learning. Then in the afternoons, they venture outside of their schools to use what they learned. They interact with locals, investigating linguistic and cultural similarities and differences and trying out their language skills.

This interaction helps students to **Communicate Ideas**, however simple they may initially be (e.g., "Excuse me, Sir. Could you tell me how to get to _____, please?") Both productive and receptive language skills are paramount in interactions with locals.

Educator Spotlight: Meghan Schumacher
Position: French Teacher
School: West Seattle High School
City, State: Seattle, WA

How did you get involved with CIEE, and why did you continue to keep a relationship with them for your students?

I was approached by a CIEE rep in 2017, asking if I would be interested in applying to be a Global Navigator school. Normally when I was approached by a travel or study abroad company, I declined, but two things stood out for me about CIEE: the availability of scholarships, which makes this an equitable opportunity for students, and the fact that CIEE is the organization that I went abroad with as a college student in 1996. The first group of students, a group of 11, went in the summer of 2018. These students came back raving about their experience. I remember the first time one of my students told me that it was the best thing that she had ever done. Those were very powerful words for me, because I felt like my involvement in this program allowed me to make a difference for my students on a very deep level.

What makes CIEE's offerings special?

CIEE goes beyond giving students scholarships to study abroad. There are plenty of study abroad organizations with mediocre teachers and questionable housing situations. CIEE offers excellence at every level of the student experience. This includes communication with families, dynamic lessons which allow for students to deeply engage with the target language and culture, interesting and engaging excursions, daily opportunities to practice language with native speakers, free time for exploration, and enriching host family experiences.

How do you promote CIEE's programs in your classes and/or school?

I talk the programs up from the first day of school. In November, we have a full day of presentations and a parent night so that their parents can come and ask questions. In class, I seek out individual students who are a good fit for the program and encourage them to apply. I send informational emails home to families, but I also reach out individually to parents if I think a student is a good candidate, but they might need a little extra encouragement. We have an alumni club at school whose purpose is to encourage students to apply and help them with their applications. They meet weekly and help with bulletin boards, speak at the info sessions, and offer application help sessions. They also have a Google Drive with testimonials and a page with their discount referral codes. We also make sure the information is on the school website and in the principal's newsletters.

What have your students who have participated in CIEE High School Summer Abroad programs reported when they come back?

Most of the students whom I talk to have had outstanding experiences. What really speaks to this is the number of students who decide to apply to go a second time. We currently have four students who are applying again. Even though it can be challenging, students appreciate the opportunity for personal and linguistic growth and the opportunity to become more independent. It is truly a life-changing experience for many students. They know when they come back that there are so many more possibilities for their lives than what they thought before, and they have developed friendships that they seek to maintain.

How does CIEE High School Summer Abroad programs support increased global competence in students?

Students have the opportunity to learn firsthand how lifestyles are different in other places. They notice little things, like how people stand in line differently, or different customs for meals. They also notice big things, like how in France, dinner conversations get philosophical or become heated political arguments where participants enjoy political repartee. They have a better understanding of the difficulties facing different parts of the world, such as a shortage of clean water in Mexico or a deeper understanding of the historical struggles of South Africa. They feel a much greater level of confidence communicating in their second language, even if they don't feel fluent when they leave. They know they are a part of the greater world and they see a place for themselves in that world.

Former Student Spotlight: Sam Russell (former CIEE High School Summer Abroad participant)
City, State: Ann Arbor, MI

How did you get introduced to the idea of the High School Summer Abroad program with CIEE?

The idea of high school study abroad I first really considered from an introduction in class; however, the first time I had heard of the CIEE program was from a friend who had gone with them to Botswana earlier. I didn't know a lot about the program except its name, and through information in class I was able to be fully introduced to the program.

What program did you do, and what made you choose to go abroad?

I did a short summer abroad program in Rennes, France, which spanned about a month. (I can't remember if it had a specific internal name, but I do remember it was listed as the more advanced option out of those possible.) I think the main reasons I chose to go abroad were centered on personal development and language goals. While I had heard French growing up somewhat, and in school for years, I felt that I really needed a final push to get me to where I thought I'd want to go with the language. I think a lot of that goal came from wanting to live up to my family, who are all French speakers. A little further into that, I think that French helped me feel more connected to my family—and particularly both my grandparents (who'd spoken French as well). I hoped that I could match up to that by getting French straight from the source! Beyond the language specifics, I was also looking for something to test myself and prove that I could go out and "really do it," in the words I would've used then. While I had done sleepaway camps and other similar things as a kid, I felt like I wanted to push the boundary and see what I could do.

What did the program look like for you? How were your days and/or the month as a whole set up for students?

The program was structured roughly like a school month—if school were purely language-focused. We spend weekday mornings in the classroom, commuting from the homes of our host families to the school (a university, in my case). We got lessons in language, grammar, and culture from our teacher, as well as receiving small projects and the likes on the side. For lunch and the early afternoon they would let us go out and purchase a lunch with stipend money and then do a cultural activity. The notable one we had to do a lot was an interview on the street about that day's class subject. We would go to the squares and streets of downtown and see if we could get an interview in. The rest of the day was then left to us, and I spent most of that time doing various things around the city with my friends. Then I'd go home to eat dinner with my host family, chat for a long time, and then head to bed or do some schoolwork. Weekends were generally centered around activities either with the program or with our host families. The program made a good effort to show us landmarks in the area and get us exposed to people of all different backgrounds. At the end of the month, we completed a small final project, took a language assessment, and then left.

What was the experience of living with a host family like?

Living with a host family was an awesome experience, and honestly probably where I learned the most French by a landslide. I was actually most scared of living with a host family because I was really worried about the language barrier, but it proved to be a much easier time than I expected. Daily structure wasn't all that different from that back home: wake up, breakfast, school, activities, family dinner, talk, repeat! I always enjoyed our dinners and time together, because it really gave me a chance to get to know my host family. I was fortunate that my conversational skills were already decent enough to get going solidly from the beginning, so I was spared a lot of language shock. (Although I will say I did accidentally tell my family their food was bland for a month, as I didn't know that spicy was a different word from what I used. I wrote them after I figured it out and had a good laugh.) Living with my host family really allowed me to learn a lot of small things about culture and nuances in the language that I wouldn't have had the chance to learn otherwise. There is no greater conversation test and practice than living with a host family!

What would you say to a student considering a study abroad on a program such as this? Are there any tips you'd give?

You should absolutely go, no questions asked, no if, ands, or buts. It will give you more amazing experiences—for language learning and just for fun—than you can imagine. The cost can sometimes be prohibitive, but a lot of programs might be able to offer support, so don't be too discouraged! It is an experience I wish every person could have because for me it was truly formative as I became a young adult, and I hope that others would enjoy a similar experience!

As for tips, there's plenty I can say but I'll keep my list original and focused. The main things I found myself struggling with were confidence and questioning the kindness of others. People in every place I've been have been nothing but kind and helpful if you try your best, so don't worry too much about your language ability, and just go for it!

Another thing I would advise is to take even a few minutes before you leave to think about what you personally want out of it, and think of what you can do to make sure that you support that. Your personal goals might not perfectly meet the program, so if there's something you really want, you may need to do stuff on your own!

My last tip is to take as many pictures as you can (within reason… still live in the moment and all that). But being able to look back and have some fond memories is worth so much, and I'm so glad that I have so many pictures!

How does the High School Summer Abroad program support increased global competence in students?

My global competence was increased most by taking what I had learned and seen and discussed, and thinking back to my own culture and experiences. High school is such a formative time in life, and being able to understand a lot more about my cultural and personal place in the world has made me a better student, person, and I hope global citizen too.

21

Virtual Reality

My first (non-)experience with virtual reality (VR) was seeing it in the video for Aerosmith's 1993 power ballad, "Amazing." I remember thinking, "What the heck *is that*?" Oddly enough, that question, combined with a quizzical look and obligatory head tilt, is *still* the first thing that comes to mind when I see someone using VR. It's clear the user is in a reality that I am not, and I immediately wonder what that reality *is*. Where are they? What are they seeing? What are they doing? Why are they moving like that?

For world language classes, the *where* can be nearly anywhere in the world; what they're *seeing* can be landscapes, cityscapes, and people; what they're *doing* is exploring what they're interested in! VR can be an incredible tool in a world language teacher's arsenal, and it has the unique ability to fulfill gaps that we have in our own knowledge. For example, I have never been to Québec. I know some of the more famous landmarks in Québec City, and I know a handful of cultural items, but my time in Canada has thus far been limited to Ontario. So when my level 2 students read a reader that took place in Québec, my own knowledge came up short, and I was stuck. I felt like I had two options: Skip cultural info altogether or intensely research. It didn't feel professional or fair to skip it altogether, but I also didn't have the time to research as much as I wanted to.

But why did I hold on to the narrow view of the *teacher* having to disseminate knowledge to the *students*? I should've known better. I should've considered what my students have taught me for years: if I set up the right environment, they can take it from there.

Instead of telling my students about the places in the reader, I let them explore themselves. From a list of landmarks mentioned in the story, students picked what sounded most interesting to them, and with the help of our media specialist, they got to experience that landmark and the surrounding area via VR. Students could only go to the media center two at a time because we only had two VR systems, but with careful planning, it worked out beautifully. Students got to spend about ten minutes each exploring their chosen area, and they walked away with more cultural input—and input that was their choice, interest-wise—than they had before.

Equity in VR

VR systems aren't cheap and, unfortunately, this technology lands squarely in the "you get what you pay for" arena. In order to create a low-stress, high-educational-return experience for students, investing in the right equipment is fundamental to success. The good news is that because of VR's capacity to promote global education, it's a prime candidate for receiving a NEA Foundation grant.

Although it's evident that not all students can afford to travel outside of their city, state, or country, we must consider that not all students whose families *can* afford travel are even *physically able* to do so. There are many students whose physical and/or mental disabilities prevent them from either being able to travel or being able to feel comfortable while doing so. For those students, VR is a powerful tool to provide global "travel" appropriate to their needs.

Tying VR to Global Education Principles

Through VR, students are able to **Investigate the World** in interesting ways. Because VR resembles a true 3D experience, senses are heightened…just like when we physically travel! The investigation can be totally student choice (*Where do you want to go? Let's put that address into the VR system!*), or teachers can curate a more specific experience, choosing where students will explore so that it ties into specific cultural information from class.

Educator Spotlight: Matt Benson
Position: Media Specialist/Teacher Librarian
School: Poudre High School
City, State: Fort Collins, CO

What would a media specialist need to know about setting up a VR system?

The first thing to know is that there is a massive range of VR platforms. These vary greatly in terms of price as well as the quality of the experience. At the lowest level, you have a smartphone in a cardboard box and a VR app. These apps provide a low/mediocre VR experience with little interactivity from the user. At the other end of the spectrum, the VR experience is incredibly realistic, and controllers allow the user to interact in their environment. Headsets can run upward of $1000 and oftentimes require a high-end gaming PC. Although the lower-priced option may seem like the best option due to budget restrictions, the experience is just too limited and lacks the truly authentic and powerful experience. Exploring grants and other funding opportunities should definitely be considered in order to provide students with a highly immersive experience.

In what ways do you see VR being a useful tool for teachers? Does that vary by level (elementary, middle, high school, post-secondary)?

VR provides students with a learning opportunity that textbooks and videos just cannot provide. An interactive and immersive experience gives students the chance to explore parts of the world right from your classroom. With apps such as Google Earth VR, students can "walk" through the streets of Barcelona, "fly" over Dubai in a jet pack, or quietly walk the hall of the museums of Paris. Giving students the feeling of being there increases engagement, understanding, and global awareness.

What are the limitations of using VR for global "travel" experiences?

VR is a powerful simulation tool that can give students the chance to virtually see and explore the cities, art, and geography of countries they are studying. It's a learning tool with great potential, but it should not be seen as an equal substitution to traveling in real life. The people, smells, sounds, climate, and true experience of physically being in a place will likely never be equaled with VR, at least not in our lifetimes.

Also, even high-end VR limits the amount of users at a time to one student per headset. Therefore, the time required to allow all students to have a legitimate experience in the VR environment should be a consideration.

How can using VR support increased global competence in students?

VR can increase global competencies in students in many ways. First of all, through VR students can experience different cultures and perspectives. VR can transport students to locations around the world where they can learn about different cultures, customs, and ways of life. It allows them to build empathy and analyze economic diversity. Imagine students exploring the favelas of Rio and the slums of Mumbai. Students can also explore sustainability and climate change by exploring human impact on the environment. Students can witness travel through time and see the impacts firsthand.

Also, as the quality of VR increases and the experiences become more immersive, apps that allow students to practice language skills are an incredible tool. VR can be used to create immersive language-learning experiences which allow language learners to practice their skills in a realistic and engaging way—almost like being in a language immersion program in a foreign country.

Finally, VR can be a great equalizer for students with financial or family situations that limit the chances of travel. VR makes "traveling" globally more accessible to students and provides educational opportunities that may not otherwise be available.

22

Forging Your Own Path

Global education—the resources, the strategies, and the outcomes—can be quite contagious, particularly among globally minded educators. Noah Zeichner is a Spanish and Social Studies teacher in Washington, and with his students, he has led the charge for global education in a BIG way.

Several years ago, one of Noah's students, Molly, received a scholarship to attend the Aspen Ideas Festival. Twelve students were selected from a national pool, and each student got to bring a teacher with them to the event. Molly chose Noah.

Revved up on inspiration and ideas after learning from and interacting with some of the biggest movers and shakers, thought leaders, artists, and business minds around, the scholarship recipients were tasked with setting up a project on their own turf.

At home, the pair got to work! In the early years of the project, it was low cost, and school-wide. They began with the question, "What do global issues look like?" and decided to call their project World Water Week. (World Water Day is March 22.) Molly and Noah were motivated by the global concept of water because of a trip to Guatemala during which they witnessed a drip line system using two-liter bottles. Their theme, they figured, could easily be interdisciplinary, and at an international school, they knew they could bring in a global approach.

The World Water Week festival at Chief Sealth International High School included a full-day student conference. During the day, there were 20–30 different sessions that classes could sign up to attend, and at night there was a keynote speaker for the entire community. Subthemes present in the sessions included water-related issues such as global water scarcity, plastic pollution, toilets, and food shortages. Throughout the week, there were assemblies and school-wide lessons.

Molly and Noah worked with a local arts organization to cross-promote events, and the organizing team raised money for speakers and applied for grants. One year, they were able to fly in the founder of the World Toilet Organization from Singapore to give the keynote address! There was professional development offered for teachers going into World Water Week so that the conference could truly be interdisciplinary and have participation and buy-in from the entire school.

After four successful years of World Water Week, Noah and his students decided to expand the festival into an international youth conference that focused not just on water but on a wide range of global issues. By this point, the high school had teamed up with the Global Issues Network. This organization supports youth-led conferences around the world, and Chief Sealth International High School adapted their structure to organize the conference. Through this partnership, the Washington Global Issues Network (WAGIN) Conference truly had a global reach. In 2019, for example, there were student attendees from Mexico, South Korea, and Cuba! The school charged a registration fee of $40 per student to attend. The total budget grew to $7,000–8,000, half of which was food. Friday included lunch and dinner, and Saturday included lunch.

Four years of World Water Week were followed by six years of global issues conferences. But wait...how does this *happen*? How does Señor Zeichner have time to teach *and* plan week-long festivals and youth-led conferences that draw in participants and speakers from all over the world?

The answer lies in teamwork.

Noah describes what the WAGIN Conference morphed into as a "Leadership Machine." There is a core team of students (four to five) who plan with Noah, and they meet once a week during lunch or even in the evening via Zoom. Then there are other committees, each mentored by a teacher: fundraising, communications, and food. The conference sessions are presented by student teams, and the various teams and committees start planning in September for a March event that was truly school-wide and interdisciplinary. The conference also included a Resource Fair, and local organizations were invited (by students) to have a table.

A youth-led, international conference may not be on most teachers' radars. It wasn't for Noah either—not initially. This event started small and without a budget; it was an exciting challenge, but doable. With full-school buy-in and support, the load could be spread around, and once Global Issues Network got involved, the reach and possibilities grew considerably.

So how does one start something *small*, but similar, in their own school? Noah gives two simple pieces of advice: First, pick a Sustainable Development Goal (SDG) to focus on. Second, plan a school-wide lesson around that SDG. It will develop from there.

Equity in WAGIN

The WAGIN Conference has largely been student-run with adult mentors. This allows students to drive the equitable practices in the conference. If you chose to do something similar, ask: Who are the students on the core planning team? Who are the leaders in the committees? Are we getting equitable representation from the student body?

Once there is equity in the leadership, we do the same for the speakers. Who are they? Where are they from? Do they represent a wide cross section of the global society?

Lastly, the planning team should be tasked with devising ways to make *attendance* at the conference equitable. What is the cost? Is this a deterrent? Is there a way we can offer scholarships? One simple idea is to offer a tiered registration system:

Standard Rate: I'd like to pay $40 to cover my student's conference fee.

Sponsor Rate: I'd like to pay $80 to cover my student's conference fee as well as that of a student who couldn't otherwise attend.

Tying WAGIN to Global Education Principles

The WAGIN Conference was built from the ground up. From the beginning, students set out to **Investigate the World**; specifically, they investigate how the topic of water touches the entire globe.

Through the speakers, attendees are able to **Recognize Perspectives**. Students present as well, which means they are **Communicating Ideas** with diverse audiences.

The conference itself is a massive step in **Taking Action** to improve conditions. The students and teachers work together to include the local/regional area *as well as* bringing in a global audience and network of expertise, so after attendees return home, the conference's call to action can spread further yet.

SECTION 4
The Way Forward

23

Increasing Our Own Global Competence

As excited as I was to learn about the field of global education, there was—and still remains—a persistent nagging in the back of my mind: *I need to learn more! I need to travel more! I need to make more global connections myself if I am to educate my students in an authentic way!*

While it's true that teachers need to increase their own global competence, it's also true that it can't be achieved in one fell swoop. Global competence is not an endpoint; rather, it's a process of continual growth and education. There will be no "I've arrived!", only ever an "I'm on the path."

The following are a few highlights of what is available for teachers in their quest to travel more, increase global competence, and learn more about global education. This list is not in any way exhaustive, and language professionals will surely think of more resources. As you do, please share them with colleagues and become part of the global education conversation in your schools and online.

Read

Simple, inexpensive, and obvious, educating ourselves through reading will never go out of style. Certainly in a post-pandemic world, virtual book clubs have popped up all over! The

International Center for Language Studies (ICLS), for example, hosts a free Language Teacher Book Club. While not all the books are focused on global competence, they *are* focused on world language learning and education.

The University of Minnesota offers a low-cost, online book club for educators as well. The books are typically middle grade or young adult, and they are largely written by authors of color.

Currently, you're holding the only book about global education that is specific to the world language context. There are, however, many books about global education, in general. Among them:

At School in the World: Developing Globally Engaged Teachers by Carine Ullom

Global Education Guidebook: Humanizing K-12 Classrooms Worldwide through Equitable Partnerships by Jennifer D. Klein

The Global Education Toolkit for Elementary Learners by Homa Sabet Tavangar and Becky Mladic-Morales

Educating Students to Improve the World by Fernando M. Reimers

12 Lessons to Open Classrooms and Minds to the World by Fernando M. Reimers

One Student at a Time: Leading the Global Education Movement by Fernando M. Reimers

Empowering Students to Improve the World in Sixty Lessons by Fernando M. Reimers

Listen

The NEA Foundation has a podcast called "Up Close with Sara Sneed." The podcast champions public education, and the Foundation is a fierce and vocal advocate of global education. Additionally, the "Leading Equity Podcast" with Dr. Sheldon L. Eakins is a first-rate resource for learning how to do this work in a way that advances the education of all students.

Global Learning Fellowship

The NEA Foundation funds this competitive fellowship whose goals include giving teachers the knowledge and skills necessary to use a global education approach in their classrooms and to advocate for global education in their local contexts. The year-long fellowship includes a weekend in Washington D.C. with all of the fellows, online webinars throughout the year, and a culminating field study abroad. During the field study, the fellows learn about the educational systems and unique historical context of that country. I was a NEA Global Learning fellow with the class of 2018, and it remains the most life-changing professional development I've ever undertaken.

Teachers for Global Classrooms

Similar to the Global Learning Fellowship (GLF), Fulbright's Teachers for Global Classrooms (TGC) is also highly competitive and includes year-long professional development that concludes with a field study abroad. The GLF brings all teachers to the same field study country, but this Fulbright TGC program sends teachers in small groups to a variety of locations. The Facebook group "Fulbright Teacher Exchange Applicants" is worthwhile for anyone applying for a short-term program (such as TGC) or a longer Fulbright teaching program.

Global Education 101

This is a free course offered by the U.S. Department of State, and it offers Continuing Education Units (CEUs) upon completion. The course, though short, is an excellent introduction to global education.

Pulitzer Center Teacher Fellowship

This is a *paid* fellowship in which teachers of grades 4–12 develop units with other educators using global education principles in an effort to increase global competency and empathy.

National Geographic

The Grosvenor Teacher Fellowship is another field study-based fellowship, and National Geographic funds this exemplary opportunity for teachers to increase geographic awareness and inspire students to take action to create a more sustainable, connected world.

National Geographic also has a wide array of free, high-quality professional development courses for educators on their website.

Travel with Students

If you take your own students abroad, some companies (such as Education First, featured in Chapter 16) will send new group leaders on a free training tour. This tour could be either in your target language-speaking world or outside of it.

CIEE (Chapter 20) is tremendous for students, but it also provides travel opportunities for teachers. For any teacher who has ten or more students from their school participate in a high school summer abroad program in a given summer, CIEE will send that teacher abroad to check out one of their programs in full swing. Additionally, CIEE hires teachers to lead their summer abroad programs.

Fund for Teachers

Have you found a program that will increase your global competence or your knowledge of global education, but you need financial support to make it happen? Fund for Teachers has grants that will support teachers in doing just that!

The University of North Carolina at Chapel Hill World View

The University of North Carolina at Chapel Hill (UNC)'s World View program is dedicated to global education and providing educators with resources and professional development to further the mission of student success in an interconnected world. They offer programs in person and virtually, as well as their own fellowship and library of resources.

The Asia Society and World Savvy

The two organizations (introduced in Chapter 1), the Asia Society and World Savvy, are leaders in the field of global education. Both offer extensive resources on their websites, ranging from information on global education (perfect for the beginner) to their well-developed partnerships and programs. The Asia Society and World Savvy are well connected to others doing the work, so they are both logical places to start when digging into global education work.

Social Media

Join social media groups and follow organizations and hashtags that champion global education. Many of the organizations listed in this chapter have a strong social media presence and are worth following.

NEA Foundation Grants

Do you already have an idea to increase global competence in your school or classroom? Apply for a grant with the NEA Foundation! They are leaders in their commitment to global education, and they make an effort to fund like-minded teachers.

Longview Foundation

This organization is steeped in passion for global education, and its Global Teacher Education (GTE) Fellowship program supports college and university teacher educators in equipping the next generation of teachers to teach with a global lens. Upon completion of the fellowship in global education, these teacher educators receive a stipend for their work.

The Longview Foundation also offers grants that can support the global education work of individual PK-12 teachers or their districts.

Harvard Graduate School of Education

Harvard Graduate School of Education (HGSE) is another strong leader in the field of global education. It offers professional development for teachers at a range of price points. Among its offerings are the "Educating Global Citizens" and "Think Tank on Global Education" programs. The former provides a firm foundation in the work, and the latter allows participants to more actively engage with educators around the world who are committed to this work.

Global Exploration for Educators Organization (GEEO)

While Global Exploration for Educators Organization (GEEO) doesn't offer free travel, it does offer substantial discounts for K-12, university, and retired teachers and administrators. They also offer free curriculum that may be valuable to your classroom, and through travel with them, you can earn graduate credit.

Language-Specific Support

World language teachers can also find support for this work through language-specific organizations. Check into your language's national organization, as well as foreign organizations in North America whose mission is to further the study of their country's language to see what opportunities are available for teachers. For instance, the Qatar Foundation funds grants for individual teachers and for schools to support Arabic language programs.

24

Converting the Naysayers

No matter the level of excitement, the soundness of the argument, or the expertise behind the movement, there will always be naysayers. The greatest minds in history all had them, and education movements aren't exempt from them either. There will always be "that guy"—that parent, board member, administrator, community member, or even student—who is slow to get on board and is suspicious of anything deviating from their "norm."

Bear in mind, however, that not all naysayers have a goal of shooting down everything educators try. Some do, true, but others may simply not understand and may genuinely be trying to learn. We can get further, faster, if we assume positive intent, so here are a few tips to use in your conversations about bringing global education into your setting.

Show Interest and Make Others Feel Important

Humans naturally enjoy feeling important; we like believing our ideas and opinions matter. So why not make the (perceived) naysayer feel important before the global education conversation even starts? Sometimes, we don't know the conversation is coming up, but when we do, we need to arrive having done our homework. Who are we talking to, and what is important to them? What successes have they had that we can bring up and congratulate them on? What skills do they have that we can (genuinely) say we admire and would love to use? Who might we know in common—a name we can use to establish a connection? We can take the lead in the conversation and steer it more skillfully when we set up a solid foundation of friendly ground first, but this needs to be done from a place of sincerity. When we find areas in which we truly connect or have an honest interest or curiosity, it's a conversational skill to use those.

Get Them Saying "Yes"

In addition to the strategy above, Dale Carnegie, in *How to Win Friends and Influence People,* also notes the importance of getting others to say "yes" before venturing in with what we want from that person. He said that a "yes" on any number of topics—which don't even have to have anything to do with *your* topic—sets the scene for *your* topic also receiving a "yes."

Ask Questions

Teachers are trained to ask the right questions. We are trained to ask questions to support students in finding the answer (the answer *we* already know) on their own, rather than us merely giving it to them. Keep asking questions until you find a "hook"— that "in" that allows you to say, "So you're saying you want ____ and that ____ is important to you. That's so interesting because there's a resource I know of that actually helps students with that exact issue. Are you familiar with ____? I'm so excited because it sounds like it would support exactly what you want!"

Language Matters

Language teachers know the power of words. There's one word, however, we would do well to steer clear of while doing the work of global education: change.

"Change" is a polarizing word. When a change is proposed, there are generally two main camps: those heavily *in favor* and those vehemently *opposed*. Instead, let's use language that is simultaneously accurate and non-polarizing. My favorite option is *grow/growth*. Growth implies forward movement, without any implied pace, but change commonly sparks the idea of a 180-degree turn. It's easy for people to argue against *change*, but it's difficult for those same people to say that *growth* is negative.

Instead of: We need to change education.
We say: Let's discuss how we can grow.
Instead of: I'm proposing a change to the curriculum.
We say: What we currently have is ripe for some powerful growth.

During the first part of the conversation, attempt to do more of the listening and less of the talking. Make it your goal to get the other party to talk and tell their story. When we use the right language, show interest, and ask the right questions, we can find that they, too, had a "spark"—a moment in another country (or city, or state…) that flipped a switch for them. Chances are, they'd love to talk about it! Then you can go on to agree with how wonderful that experience was, and how they (yes, *they*) are so correct that if we created the right environment, students could feel that same way!

On occasion, we may not have the time to implement the strategies above, or we may be blindsided by a question out of the blue. The following are comments you may hear from those who have reservations about your work in global education, paired with talking points to use in your response.

This Sounds Too Expensive

Start with ideas that are free or low cost to get others on board. Section 2 provides many resources, but Section 3 includes ideas for taking the higher-cost strategies and making them accessible. Remember, global education is not something that can be adapted in a day, nor does it have an endpoint; it's a lifelong journey. To that end, it doesn't matter how seemingly "small" the start is.

This is a prime opportunity to put the naysayer in the driver's seat. Explain some of the low-cost strategies and resources, and ask their opinion: "I value you as a member of our community. I'm drawn to all of the resources I mentioned, but you have a unique viewpoint that I don't. I'm so curious to know what jumps out at you as interesting. I'd like to start with that!" (Remember, people like to feel important.)

Why Focus Globally? What Does That Have to Do with Me and My Child?

Here, data can be highly useful, and it's worthwhile to always be armed with some of the latest data. For instance, we can point out that globalization has changed jobs, and educators need to prepare student for jobs of the future. Over 40 million U.S. jobs are tied to international trade, and we can ask, "Is it important to you to see international trade flourish?" (*Yes, of course…*) "Shouldn't we try to maximize our trade power by having a workforce skilled in international competence?" (*Well, yes…*) "Do you want to pay privately for the next generation of workers to develop this skill?" (*No…*) "So it feels like you support the idea of it being part of a free, public education?" (*Yes, that seems right.*)

If the person you're talking to is a parent, ask them about their dreams for their child. We would be hard-pressed to find a parent who didn't want their child to have a better life and more opportunities than them. That's what global education can provide: opportunities! Many parents dream of their child "getting out" of the place they, their parents, and their parents' parents grew up in. They dream of their child breaking free and blazing their own trail. Global education equips students to do just that. Conversely, there are also parents who are afraid of their child leaving and never coming home. To those parents, we can point out that if the child does leave to explore the world—and just for a time—they can come back and support the growth of their home community in a way that those before them never have been able to.

This Is Anti-American!

Once again, data is useful. There are a multitude of resources available to determine the United States' top trading partners, and this information does routinely shift, but sources typically point to one or, at most, two of those top ten countries being English-speaking. Of the one or two countries, one of them (Canada) is only *partially* English-speaking. An argument, then, is that if we want to further American business interests, we need to cultivate a globally competent workforce. Disney lost billions of dollars with Euro Disney's failed initial implementation, largely due to lack of global competence and cultural knowledge. Global education will advance financial priorities in our businesses and capitalist system.

Global education is also a national safety issue. What could make us more secure than an entire generation of young leaders establishing connections and friendships all across the globe? And education is significantly more fiscally responsible than military action! Instilling global competence in our young people creates a safer United States because the more we know and understand about the world, the safer we are in it; we're better prepared.

In his memoir *Surrender*, U2's front man, Bono, recounts at length his work with the U.S. government on debt relief for the world's poorest countries and on financial support for the African AIDS crisis. He details a conversation he had with billionaire investor Warren Buffet in which the latter told him, "Don't appeal to the conscience of America. Appeal to the greatness of America. That's how you'll get the job done." And the strategy worked…to the tune of $100 billion in aid. The same strategy can be used here. Global educators can assert, "Much of the rest of the developed world already has a more global stance. America wasn't built to be behind—we were built to lead. From the beginning, we set an example. We set an example for freedom, and it inspired the French to follow with their own revolution! Revolutionary trailblazers in global education are *here*. Let's use their expertise to put America on top and leading this charge! What's more American than leadership?"

You, personally, may not believe that a capitalist approach is the right one, and you may not believe in the perceived greatness of America. You can agree or disagree; it is a moot point. What's crucial to recognize is that anyone arguing that global education is "anti-American" *may* believe those things. Using the tips above does not mean you agree with their stance. Rather, it means that you *know how to speak their language*. It means that you see how what they want and what you want are actually linked and that you are skilled enough to explain that in a way they can relate to.

The tips and strategies above all boil down to *language*, and command of language is the world language teacher's superpower. Let's not be afraid to use it.

25

Igniting the Spark

I'm originally from the Minneapolis area. If you've never been there, there's one fact to know about us: Prince is a part of our Minnesota identity. Prince, famously, didn't like to talk about his songs or albums once he released them, despite their brilliance. It was done. It was over. And he no longer found it interesting. He wanted to talk about the future and where the music was *going*.

I feel the same way about education. I want to focus on the future, and **the future is global education**.

Global education involves Investigating the World, Recognizing Perspectives, Communicating Ideas, and Taking Action (Asia Society). It includes Behaviors, Skills, Values, and Attitudes that support global competence (World Savvy). The Sustainable Development Goals and the trait of empathy are woven throughout the curriculum, and globally competent teachers are the indispensable guides in this work. It all boils down to this:

> Global education isn't learning *about* the world; it is learning *with* and *from* the world.

Because of our education, experience, and expertise, world language teachers are undoubtedly best suited to lead. We speak at least two languages, and we have been trained to infuse culture into our work. We love to travel more than any other teacher group, seeing the world as our playground and its people as friends we simply haven't met yet. Our very nature is one of cultural curiosity, and we aren't afraid to make mistakes—in fact, we do so regularly with accents and translation blunders, and we have no problem correcting the mistake and moving on.

When considering the ideas, strategies, and resources for students and teachers within these chapters, it's imperative not to frame our questions with *"Can* I do these things?"—because of course we can!—but instead with *"How* can I do these things?" The former proposes a limiting binary of can or can't, yes or no, doing the work or not doing the work. The latter takes it as a given that yes, you *can* do the work; it's simply a question of *how*.

Start by mapping out a global connection plan, version 1.0, and recognize that it will evolve. First consider what you already do in your classrooms, and follow that with what feels exciting to try and what feels like an easy fit. The process will evolve naturally, but if you partner with like-minded educators, the growth potential raises exponentially. Lastly, don't forget that you are also a piece of the puzzle. When you engage in experiences that elevate your own global competence, your students will benefit from it.

In addition to the *how*, there is also the *why*. The personal why is that at some point we had a global experience that created a fundamental shift in our minds and hearts. A spark was ignited in our very core, and we understand its power in our development. The universal why is that, more than ever, the problems that exist in our world are *global* problems, and they require *global* solutions.

I hope you are inspired by the potential and invigorated by the challenge within these pages. Global education is creating the next generation of world shapers and leaders. We may not see minds and hearts changed while a student is in our classroom, but everyone engaged in this important work should know this: We're igniting a spark.

Resources

Chapter 1
Book: *Educating for Global Competence: Preparing Our Youth to Engage the World* by Veronica Boix Mansilla & Anthony Jackson: https://asiasociety.org/files/book-globalcompetence.pdf
Global Competence Outcomes & Rubrics: https://asiasociety.org/education/leadership-global-competence
United Nations' SDGs: https://sdgs.un.org/goals
World Savvy: https://www.worldsavvy.org

Chapter 3
Language & Friendship: https://languageandfriendship.com/

Chapter 4
Poudre Library District: https://www.poudrelibraries.org/outreach/world-storytimes

Chapter 6
Empatico: https://empatico.org/
Stevens Initiative: https://www.stevensinitiative.org/

Chapter 7
ePals: https://www.epals.com/

Chapter 10
Climate Action: https://youtu.be/R7g-HCoeSlw
Climate Change: https://www.youtube.com/watch?v=m9pw8AjjjLE&t=24s
Climate Change: https://www.youtube.com/watch?v=3OtOl3pHNxk&t=21s
Climate Change: https://youtu.be/9awJYgYrgoU
Education Equality: https://www.youtube.com/watch?v=gBRWPsq7410
Education Equity: https://www.youtube.com/watch?v=2BhTPiRiMZM
Fossil Fuels: https://www.youtube.com/watch?v=Ex1JqSXG-Ig&t=43s
Gender Equality: https://www.youtube.com/watch?v=CZRJejBEMbg&t=46s

Gender Equity: https://youtu.be/MhPeENx2ydU
Gender Equity: https://youtu.be/qQxftk9kD7s
Global Heath Grisel: https://youtu.be/QgU7DlfqCTA
Good Health & Well Being: https://www.youtube.com/watch?v=wuX3pjE38Es&t=38s
Hunger: https://www.youtube.com/watch?v=aCilBJm0Xl0&t=4s
Life on Land (collaboration w/ 5th grade class from Ohio): https://www.youtube.com/watch?v=sLyJv7Y9bJI&t=15s
Libyan Slaves: https://www.youtube.com/watch?v=NXfT_z3caRw&t=45s
Peace and Justice: https://www.miamiseniorhigh.org/apps/video/watch.jsp?v=10027956
Pollution: https://youtu.be/2LCFqtCxPUU
Pollution: https://www.youtube.com/watch?v=aXC9D0esDf8&t=30s
Poverty in Africa: https://www.youtube.com/watch?v=0YAc_mUlsvU
Poverty in Honduras: https://youtu.be/bClRqSGD83s
Poverty in Nicaragua: https://www.youtube.com/watch?v=sJX_zgIT0GE&t=46s
School Violence (collaboration w/ Emma Smith): https://youtu.be/xzCMBLsO2Xk
School Violence, #NeverAgain, #ItsTime (collaboration w/ Emma Smith): https://www.youtube.com/watch?v=vfzxDqjwE30&t=37s
Violence: https://www.youtube.com/watch?v=lDEUSjRzX04&t=30s
War & Poverty: https://www.youtube.com/watch?v=gGUJ2tRPsrM
Water in Haiti (Spanish version): https://www.youtube.com/watch?v=5pOxdh3rnos&t=56s
Water Issues in Haiti (Spanish Version): https://www.youtube.com/watch?v=PCjR2AY2ae0
World Poverty: https://www.youtube.com/watch?v=AZN5e0FHB-s&t=73s

Chapter 12
Radio Garden: http://radio.garden
Window Swap: https://www.window-swap.com/Window

Chapter 13
City Walks: https://citywalks.live/
Radiooooo: https://radiooooo.com/

Chapter 14
News in Slow _____ : https://www.newsinslow.com/

Chapter 15
United Nations' SDGs: https://sdgs.un.org/goals

Chapter 16
EF Tours: https://www.eftours.com/

Chapter 17
Concordia Language Villages: http://www.concordialanguagevillages.org/

Chapter 18
Global Storybooks: https://globalstorybooks.net/
NEA Foundation Grants: https://www.neafoundation.org/educator-grants-and-fellowships/

Chapter 19
Camp Hope: https://allchildren.org/our-work/camp-hope/
Global Leaders: https://www.globalleadersinc.org/
Global Volunteers: https://globalvolunteers.org/

Chapter 20
AFS: https://afs.org/
CIEE High School Summer Abroad: https://www.ciee.org/go-abroad/high-school-study-abroad/summer

Chapter 22
Global Issues Network: https://globalissuesnetwork.org/
WAGIN '22: https://globalissuesnetwork.org/wagin2022/

Chapter 23
Fund for Teachers: https://www.fundforteachers.org/
GEEO: https://geeo.org/
Global Education 101: https://teacherexchanges.catalog.instructure.com/courses/global-education-101
Global Learning Fellowship: https://www.neafoundation.org/educator-grants-and-fellowships/global-learning-fellowship/
Grosvenor Teacher Fellowship: https://www.nationalgeographic.org/education/professional-development/grosvenor-teacher-fellows/
HGSE Educating Global Citizens: https://www.gse.harvard.edu/ppe/program/educating-global-citizens
HGSE Think Tank on Global Education: https://www.gse.harvard.edu/ppe/program/think-tank-global-education

ICLS: https://www.icls.edu/
Longview Foundation: https://longviewfdn.org/
National Geographic Professional Development: https://www.nationalgeographic.org/education/professional-development/courses/
NEA Foundation Grants: https://www.neafoundation.org/educator-grants-and-fellowships/
Pulitzer Center Teacher Fellowship: https://pulitzercenter.org/teacher-fellowship
Qatar Foundation: https://www.qfi.org/
Teachers for Global Classrooms: https://www.fulbrightteacherexchanges.org/programs/tgc/
UNC World View: https://worldview.unc.edu/
University of Minnesota Book Club: https://cla.umn.edu/global-studies/outreach-engagement/professional-development-educators/book-clubs-k-12-educators

For Product Safety Concerns and Information please contact our EU representative GPSR@taylorandfrancis.com
Taylor & Francis Verlag GmbH, Kaufingerstraße 24, 80331 München, Germany

www.ingramcontent.com/pod-product-compliance
Lightning Source LLC
Chambersburg PA
CBHW050637300426
44112CB00012B/1831